MODELLING IRISH RAILWAY

STEPHEN JOHNSON & ALAN O'ROURKE

MIDLAND
An imprint of
Ian Allan Publishing

CONTENTS

Chapter

1	Historical Background	3
2	Scales & Gauges	9
3	Modelling The Broad Gauge	13
4	Layouts	32
5	Signalling & Operation	42
6	The Narrow Gauge	50
7	Modelling In Finescale	63
8	Gallery	68
Appendix 1	Irish Model Maunfacturers	85
Appendix 2	Wheel and Track Standards	86
Appendix 3	Sources of Information	87

Modelling Irish Railways

ISBN 1 85780 185 7

Published in 2004 by
Midland Publishing,
4 Watling Drive, Hinckley
LE10 3EY, England
Tel: 01455 254490, Fax: 01455 254495
E-mail: midlandbooks@compuserve.com

Design concept and layout
© Midland Publishing
and Stephen Thompson Associates.

Midland Publishing
is an imprint of Ian Allan Publishing

Printed in England by
Ian Allan Printing Ltd, Hersham, Surrey, KT12 4RG

Front cover photographs:

Top: **GNR(I) 'SG2' class 0-6-0 No 16 approaches the junction with a car train on Harry Mulholland's 7mm Knockmore Junction layout.**

Lower left: **The distinctive red and cream livery of the County Donegal narrow gauge is seen on Charles Insley's 3mm scale, Cahir Patrick layout.** Both, Tony Wright, courtesy British Railway Modelling

Front cover photographs continued:

Lower right: **CIE '071' class General Motors diesel locomotive No 087 and a similar locomotive in NIR livery, No 111 Great Northern pose at the station throat on Stephen Johnson's Dunmore & Fidlin layout.** Stephen Johnson

Title page photograph:

GNR(I) railcar D stands in the bay platform on Tony Miles' Adavoyle Junction layout. Tony Wright, courtesy British Railway Modelling

Below: **Belfast & County Down Railway 0-6-0 No 4 is seen at work on Colm Flanigan's OO gauge Newcastle layout.** Tony Wright, courtesy British Railway Modelling

Acknowledgements

The authors would like to acknowledge and thank the following for their help and contributions in writing this book: Denis Bates, John Brennan, Harry Byrne, Joe Cassells, Roger Crombleholme, Andy Cundick, Hugh Dougherty, Ken Elliott, Tom Ferris, Ian Lawrence, Robin Linsley, David Malone, Ian McNally, Fergal Noonan, Patrick O'Sullivan, Neil Ramsay, Bill Scott, Peter Swift and Paul Taylor.

CHAPTER 1

HISTORICAL BACKGROUND

Paradoxically, in Ireland model railways may have a slightly longer history than the real thing. Dublin got a railway in 1834 (two years ahead of London) linking the city centre with the port of Kingstown, and in 1830 the promoters had commissioned plans, pictures and a model of part of the proposed line to persuade landowners to sell them property for its construction. The early lines certainly had not heard of 'ISO-9000' standards, and within certain limits defined in the parliamentary act of incorporation, were allowed to choose their own gauge. In England, there were two main schools: the Stephensons and their followers favouring 4ft 8½in; Brunel championing his broad gauge of 7ft 0¼in. The Kingstown line had been built to the English standard gauge of 4ft 8½in.

However, in 1839, the Ulster Railway opened the first section of its line from Belfast to Lisburn to the gauge of 6ft 2in, reaching Portadown in 1842. This was the gauge laid down by a government appointed commission who were asked to establish the best gauge for Ireland. Whilst the UR built its line in accordance with the commission's report, the Dublin & Drogheda Railway ignored it and planned to build its line, which would have been the southern part of an eventual through route from Dublin to Belfast, to a gauge of 5ft 2in. With the incorporation of the Dublin & Belfast Junction Railway in 1845, whose line would link the UR and the D&D, a major problem was looming. The Board of Trade was called in to arbitrate and determined that the standard gauge for Ireland should be 5ft 3in. This was confirmed by parliament in 1846. This gauge, although unusual, is not quite unique to Ireland and can also be found in Australia, India and South America. As we will discuss in Chapter 2, it causes some problems for modellers.

At the dawn of the railway age, Ireland did not look a propitious place for the new technology: it lacked both the capital to build the lines and areas of manufacturing or mining to provide the goods traffic. There had been a modest canal building age, and most large towns were by then served by coastal or inland navigations. In 1838 the Railway Commissioners for Ireland envisaged two trunk routes from Dublin. One would run north to Belfast, but well inland of the line we have now, with branches to Coleraine and Derry. The other ran south to Cork, fairly close to the route later taken by the Great Southern & Western Railway. No line to the west (as later built by the Midland Great Western Railway) was planned, the existing Grand and Royal Canals were deemed adequate for the traffic on offer. However, by 1860, the core of the Irish network was built, with lines linking Dublin to Waterford, Cork, Tralee, Limerick, Galway, Derry and Belfast. The first portions of the routes to Wexford, Sligo and Mayo were open, Belfast and Derry had their first direct link in place, and a network of local lines, especially in the north-east, was evolving. Almost from the beginning, raising capital was problematic compared to financing lines across the Irish Sea, which had more obvious potential. Later, the government encouraged the extension of lines to remoter parts of the country with loans and grants and devices like baronial guarantees, the latter a subsidy from ratepayers in districts served by the lines, who underwrote a return of typically 4-5% on the capital employed to build the railway. Initially these baronial guarantees were restricted to narrow gauge schemes which generally cost less to build. This was an encouragement to the spread of what became Ireland's second gauge of 3ft. Although a number of railways possessed, or even built, their own locomotives and rolling stock, there were always some lesser concerns for which such provision was not economic, which entered into 'working agreements' with their larger neighbours, who provided the trains for either a percentage of the receipts or mileage charges. For most of the 19th century, about half of the Irish lines were worked by their larger neighbours. As in the rest of the British Isles, there was a tendency for the smaller companies to be absorbed by or amalgamated with the bigger companies.

As mentioned earlier, a network of narrow gauge lines also developed. The first 3ft gauge line to use steam power opened in 1873 to tap iron ore deposits in County Antrim. Over the next 30-odd years, a series of narrow gauge lines opened for public traffic, largely serving remote areas such as the western seaboard counties of Kerry, Clare and Donegal. Here, the traffic could not support a broad gauge route, and the smaller gauge allowed economies in construction and engineering, in return for tighter rules on axle loading and speed. There were also a number of 5ft 3in gauge light railways, where money was saved by using less exacting standards of engineering than on the main lines. The narrow gauge lines have always exerted their own charm for modellers, and we will return to them in Chapter 6.

By the early 20th century, five large companies had emerged. The Great Southern & Western Railway (GSWR) was far and away Ireland's largest railway company, having just augmented its routes by absorbing the Waterford, Limerick & Western Railway (WLWR) and the Waterford & Central Ireland Railway (WCIR), and becoming the English Great Western Railway's partner in the Fishguard & Rosslare Railways & Harbours Company (FRRH). From Dublin, its main line ran south-west to Cork and Queenstown (Cobh from 1920), with secondary routes to Killarney, Tralee, Limerick, Waterford and Athlone. It also had cross country lines from Rosslare to Waterford and Mallow, and from Waterford all the way to Sligo via Limerick, Athenry and Claremorris.

The Great Northern Railway of Ireland (with an 'I' in brackets to distinguish it from its English namesake) had emerged in 1876, as an amalgamation of four older companies, who provided a network of lines connecting Dublin, Derry and Belfast, with various branches some built by other smaller concerns. The GNR(I) was destined to have a long independent existence, but an undignified end.

The Midland Great Western Railway (MGWR) had three main routes, from Dublin to Galway, Sligo and Mayo, and a collection of secondary routes and branches, some unwillingly acquired (the Midland board tended to view branches as parasites rather than feeders of its trunk routes), some built with government loans. It had a long quarrel with the GSWR over spheres of influence in the centre of Ireland and the ultimate fate of the Waterford, Limerick & Western Railway. Colloquially it

was called the 'most Irish of lines', partly due to the distinctive designs of its engineer Martin Atock, who until the closing years of the nineteenth century built his tender engines with characteristic bell-mouthed chimneys and cabs with turned up roofs ('the fly away cab'), and his coaches with external beading rather than the more common ornate panelling.

The Belfast & Northern Counties Railway was another amalgamation of several smaller concerns, provided a second route from Belfast to Derry, lines to Magherafelt, Draperstown, Larne and Dungiven and operated several narrow gauge branches. It was bought by the English Midland Railway in 1903 which in turn became part of the London, Midland & Scottish Railway in 1923. The Midland lines in Ireland were managed locally by an organisation based in Belfast known as the Northern Counties Committee (NCC). In 1906, the MR, along with the GNR(I), acquired the County Donegal narrow gauge system. Particularly from the 1920s on, the locomotives and rolling stock acquired a decidedly 'Derby style' which can help the modeller by allowing the adaptation of kits and components designed for LMS prototypes.

The Dublin & South Eastern Railway (DSER), to give it its final title, had the biggest suburban traffic of all the Irish companies with two routes from Dublin to Bray, one incorporating the original works of the Dublin & Kingstown Railway buried under seventy years of development and change. The D&K actually continued to exist until 1925, but latterly about its only job was to collect the rent from the DSER and declare a dividend. The southern portion of the DSER was more typical of Ireland, a single track route to Wexford with few trains serving agricultural towns, a branch to Shillelagh and a steeply graded line to Waterford. The DSER marks the transition from the major to the minor companies, one wag remarking that even it

Opposite page: **Two fine models from one of the early pioneers of Irish railway modelling, the late Drew Donaldson.**

Top: **CIÉ D15 class 4-4-0 No 296 was modelled in 7mm scale in 1973. Drew only saw the engine in service once at Limerick in 1940, and was told she was very free steaming. The model is powered, like many of Drew's, by a Hornby No 2 mechanism. As this does not project very far into the cab, he was able to add a dummy reversing wheel and screw.**

Below: **When in 1968, Drew took his demonstration layout to the Inchicore works open day, several railwaymen commented on the absence of a CIÉ B2 class 4-6-0. Within a year, Drew had filled the gap in his stud with this model of No 409. The story goes that the same enginemen, at the next open day said 'But you haven't got a Woolwich.' The B2 class were built as four-cylinder machines to reduce hammer blow to track and bridges, but were much better runners after rebuilding as two-cylinder machines. No 409 was one that had a less extensive rebuild, with the frames renewed only in front of the leading coupled axle, producing an asymmetric footplate. In 1939, she was fitted with an experimental variable orifice blast-pipe, which reduced back-pressure, and produced brilliant performance at the expense of economy. Drew's model shows her in final form with a K-class boiler. Even in the last days of steam, she was a star performer, delivering sterling work on the Cork mails and the Radio trains.** Both, courtesy W T Scott and J Cassells

was not quite sure if it was 'the tail of the whale or the head of the sprat!'

The minor broad gauge lines included independent and often highly individual companies like the Belfast & County Down and the Cork, Bandon & South Coast Railway. The Waterford & Tramore Railway, physically isolated from the rest of the network, survived as an almost pure piece of mid-Victoriana until 1925. The Sligo, Leitrim & Northern Counties Railway, by dint of its cross-border status, remained independent until closure in 1957 and the Dundalk, Newry & Greenore, was an Irish offshoot of the English London & North Western Railway, who supplied all its equipment, making it look like one of its lines mysteriously transplanted across the Irish Sea. Once you have added the narrow gauge lines and the various urban tramways, a century ago Ireland provided huge variety in terms of its railways.

In common with the English lines, the years immediately before World War 1 represented the zenith of the railways. They were labour intensive, but wages were low and unions weak; they had a near monopoly of inland transport, with the internal combustion engine still unproven technology, and the private motor car a plaything for the privileged few. Yet, even in such a favoured environment, many rural Irish lines were barely viable. World War 1 produced huge surges of military traffic, shortages of raw materials and latterly direct government control. From 1916 to 1923 political unrest saw the railways subject to attacks during the War of Independence which was followed by a civil war between the forces of the newly formed Irish Free State and those opposed to the partition of Ireland. Such attacks ranged from cutting telegraph wires and burning signal cabins, to attacks on trains, the blowing up of bridges and deliberate train wrecks. In the longer run, large scale inflation and an eight hour day for railwaymen, introduced in 1918, completely altered the economics of railways in Ireland, and increasing numbers of lorries and buses and the falling price of private motoring removed the old railway monopoly as a means of transporting goods and passengers around the country.

In 1922 Ireland was partitioned, and the GNR(I) and several minor lines found themselves burdened with the problem of operating in two states, with customs examination where they passed from Northern Ireland to the Free State. The GNR(I) crossed the border no fewer than seventeen times! The two governments adopted quite different policies on transport. In Northern Ireland, the old companies were left to struggle on as best they could. The Irish Free State convened a Railway Tribunal, and persuaded or coerced all companies whose lines lay wholly within its territory to amalgamate into the Great Southern Railways (GSR). Hardly the most prosperous of concerns, the GSR managed to preserve its network largely intact, losing only a few branches. It experimented with battery, steam and petrol railcar, and introduced a limited amount of modern electro-mechanical signalling in the Dublin area. However, it survived by financial cheese paring. It wrote off a third of its capital, keeping the smaller lines going by patching the permanent way with second hand materials and reducing speed limits to 20 or 25mph on some branches. By 1939, the arrears in maintenance on the West Cork lines alone were £14,000. Only 59 locomotives and 128 coaches were built over a 20 year period, making the GSR stock into a fascinating historical collection. A survey in 1948 showed the average age of the engines to be 51 years, with coaches 47 years old. A fifth of the locomotive stock was over 60 years old, and there were 31 classes with fewer than 10 members. After 1932, the GSR had ceased to pay dividends, and all that shareholders got was an annual First class ticket to Dublin to hear this grim news. By 1938, the company could not even pay its bills. Paradoxically, World War 2 was its succour and its downfall. Motor fuel shortages brought traffic flooding back to the railways, but latterly shortages of coal, which had almost entirely to be imported from England, reduced train services to a bare minimum on some lines and nothing at all on others, while enginemen tried to coax a working boiler pressure out of a firebox full of wood, turf, slack and 'duff' made by sticking coal dust together with bitumen.

By the end of World War 2, most Irish railway equipment was antiquated and life expired. Again the two governments pursued different policies. In the south, all inland transport was merged into a single body, Córas Iompair Éireann (CIÉ), and embarked on a rapid policy of dieselisation, including railcars, and an extensive rolling stock construction policy. In some ways, modernisation would have run more smoothly if the pace was a little slower. The first generation of diesel locomotives, which in a rebuilt form have only recently quit the scene, were far from perfect. However, from 1961 on CIÉ bought efficient General Motors units from the USA, allowing it to eliminate regular steam working in 1963. A selective programme of closures, culminating in a cull of minor and secondary lines, left a system of radial routes from Dublin, and one cross country link. In Northern Ireland, the government, established the Ulster Transport Authority (UTA) to run its buses and trains. The bus lobby dominated its management, with wholesale rail closures the result. By 1965, only the lines from Belfast to the border, Larne, Portrush and the NCC route to Londonderry survived. However, the NCC's last bequest, a fleet of modern 'WT' class 2-6-4 tank engines, and a motorway spoil hauling contract to keep them in work, meant that Northern Ireland Railways (formed when the UTA was wound up to run the few remaining railways in the province) was fated to operate the last revenue earning steam services in the British Isles.

The Great Northern weathered the 1920-1945 period better than the GSR. New steel panelled coaches appeared on its main services and some new locomotives were built. Unlike the GSR's drab livery of battleship grey engines and maroon coaches, some GNR locomotives were painted in a blue livery from the early 1930s onwards and hauled trains of varnished teak stock. It too however had elderly machines and Victorian coaches in its quieter corners, with one horse powered and one electric tramway just for variety. The resurgence of motor transport after World War 2 brought it to its knee and by 1953 the GNR(I) was bankrupt. It was taken over by a board funded by both governments. By 1957, the Northern administration was no longer willing to subsidise it, and following wholesale closures, the remains of a once great railway was divided in 1958 between CIÉ and UTA. All other cross-border lines had by then all passed into oblivion, except for the County Donegal narrow gauge, which closed the following year.

The last 20 years have seen further developments on Irish railways. The coastal section of the Dublin suburban network has been electrified in two stages, and completely new diesel hauled local services added on the inland lines. The Dublin-Belfast line has undergone major up-grading. Irish Rail, or Iarnród Éireann, which has operated railway services in the south since 1987, has acquired new fleets of railcars and main line locomotives, and substantial lengths of route have received modern signalling and continuous welded rail. The Northern network has faced problems including the threat of further closures, but these are now receding, and it has relaid the Bangor line and secured funding for a new fleet of diesel units. The government in the south has also commissioned a strategic rail review, including the possible provision of new local services. Alongside these programmes of equipping the network for the 21st century, there is a growing awareness of the historical importance of railways. For 40 years, the Railway Preservation Society of Ireland has operated preserved steam engines and coaches all over the island. The Ulster Folk & Transport Museum has moved its rail collection from cramped premises to the splendid new galleries at Cultra and special societies cater for diesel preservation. Others are working towards the restoration of closed lines. For any one wishing to explore the history briefly outlined above, there is a growing collection of high quality books, although for any budding historians, there are plenty of niches of 170 years of Irish railway history still to be explored!

The modern hobby of railway modelling has its roots in two distinct traditions: toy trains and miniature engineering. By the 1850s, one could buy crude wooden or tinplate playthings for children to push across the floor. By the end of the nineteenth century there was a fearsome new genre of miniature steam engines powered by oscillating cylinders, no doubt a source of ire to many governesses. The trail of oil and water such contraptions left across the nursery floor earned them the sobriquet of dribblers. By World War 1, various manufacturers, most prominently German, had devised a system of gauges and scales. Their products ran on rolled tinplate rails and were predominantly clockwork powered. From the 1920s onwards, increasingly smaller scales appeared, and by the time of World War 2 railway modelling in Britain was a recognised hobby, with its own press, (*Model Railway News* was established in 1925), and commercial support. Mass produced models were however usually crude representations of the prototype. From the 1950s, two developments revolutionised model railways: electric traction emerged as the favoured means of propulsion and injection plastic moulding allowed models to reach standards of realism and detail, such that many items now sold as toys are as accurate as one-off commissions of 70 years ago. The process on miniaturisation continued, down to the ultimate of Z gauge (6.5mm, ratio 1:220).

Below: **'D19' class 4-4-0 No 6 is another 7mm scale model built by Drew Donaldson in 1952, the same year that the prototype was scrapped. No 303 hauled her to Inchicore, the engine being spotlessly cleaned before its last trip by the enginemen, who were heartbroken at her withdrawal. Drew managed to photograph and measure her before her last journey. In this form she has a 'U' class saturated Belpaire boiler. Power comes from the Hornby Zulu motor, but as it had very thin gears, the model could not be used for shunting.** Photograph courtesy of W T Scott and J Cassells

Above: **Motive power from very different eras is seen at Churchtown Junction on Cyril Fry's Irish & International Railway And Tramway.**
Photo, Des McGlynn collection

The second root of model railways began with early miniatures, produced by engineering firms to demonstrate their wares. In some cases these models now provide the best knowledge we have of early locomotives and are museum pieces in their own right. Irish examples include two early Dublin & Kingstown engines: a Forrester 2-2-0 in the Straffan Collection and a 2-2-2WT in the Science Museum, London. Once railway companies had established their own works, part of the training for their apprentices often included building miniature reproductions of the company's engines and rolling stock to learn the techniques of working materials. In its purest form, this theme is represented today by large scale modellers using live steam on garden layouts.

The cult of the train-spotter, who would invest his pocket money in toy trains and possibly evolve into a serious enthusiast, never really developed in Ireland. At least one model business existed in Limerick in the 1920s, but it catered for the British market. Lacking commercial support, modelling Irish prototypes was a lonely furrow. But, from the 1930s, a few dedicated modellers set out to recreate the Irish scene in miniature, and recently this band has grown steadily, as modellers look for more unusual prototypes. One of the most prolific was Cyril Fry, who from 1936, built up a huge collection of 7mm models, as the Irish & International Railway and Tramway System (IIR&TS) which often featured in the model railway press until his death in 1972. The model occupied a specially constructed room 50ft long, built onto Fry's Dublin home, Mrs Fry assisting by painting the scenic backgrounds and manufacturing cast components. Fry focused on broad gauge models form the earliest D&K trains to the CIÉ 1950s diesels, running on 32mm (O gauge) track. His narrow gauge trains ran on 21mm track. The trams were supplied by electricity from the overhead wires. Sound and smoke effects, using a secret formula devised by Fry himself, and automatic signalling were also part of the layout. Visitors were treated to three hour demonstrations with up to seven trains in action at any one time. Fry used three-rail current supply. The tightest curves were of 3ft radius on broad gauge lines, 2ft 3in on the narrow gauge and 9in for the trams. These required some compromises, like the use of single link rigid couplings. The IIR&TS even had its own crest (quartering the Irish harp, D&K 2-2-0 *Hibernia*, the last Dublin tram and the arms of Dublin City), while the 'International' component was represented by two models of the LNWR Irish Mail set, a German Pacific and an American six-coach streamlined diesel unit. In its final form, there were 5,000 feet of track on the layout.

Fry summarised his philosophy thus: *'Complete railways have been closed in this country, as they have been on your side of the water, and all their locomotives and rolling stock scrapped, some without trace, and it is my ambition, with the help of my wife, to have, so to speak, a living record which shows in three dimensions the progress of Irish rail transport.'*

Dublin Tourism bought Fry's models from his widow, and the collection formed the nucleus of the Model Railway Museum at Malahide Castle near Dublin, which is featured elsewhere in these pages. Although most of his stock is now too fragile for regular running, his work may still be seen there, largely as static displays.

Another pioneer was the late Drew Donaldson, who concentrated on the CIÉ era of the 1950s. Whereas Fry was an early convert to electricity, Donaldson used rebuilt 'controlled' clockwork mechanisms. He once competed with a friend to see if such devices could be fitted into engines as small as the 'J30' class 0-6-0Ts (each engine took four months to build, but they were completed within hours of each other). Donaldson's approach was that of a mechanical engineer, required to provide motive power for a real railway system and some of his models, although finished to fine-scale standards, ran on carefully rebuilt and maintained clockwork mechanisms up to 50 years old. His layout was very much an operational one, with signalling and timetable operation, but practically no scenery, which he regarded as 'props', compared to locomotives as the 'heart and soul of the layout'. He once commented that: *'The visitor is likely to be astonished to see some unique engine, whose existence he had not suspected, produced from the obscurity of a shed and attached to a train. This gives great pleasure, by the way, to the operators as well, especially if the said engine gives a good account of herself, as she usually does being clockwork. Best of all was the excitement of an NCC driver watching one of his own 'Moguls' starting out with eleven bogies, two six-wheelers and four vans. (She made it easily.)'*

Drew Donaldson died in a motor accident in 1978, but a number of his models are on display at the Ulster Folk & Transport Museum at Cultra in County Down.

In the pre-plastic era, both Fry and Donaldson used tinplate and castings to make their models. They had however one huge advantage over modern modellers in that much of what they wanted to build was still running, so to get the information, they headed off to the railway with a camera and tape to measure it up. The 1960s saw growing interest in the Irish narrow gauge, using various adaptations of commercial equipment (see Chapter 6), but the gauge problem deterred modelling the broad gauge, until the 1970s when two solutions appeared in 4mm scale: using OO (16.5mm) track, as for the North Dublin Model Railway Society's model of Malahide (*Railway Modeller*, April 1973) and correct 21mm gauge (Tim Cramer, *Railway Modeller,* June 1972) and in its fullest form to P4 standards with compensated rolling stock, as exemplified by the model of Adavoyle, built by Tony Miles, David Goodwin and other members of the Merseyside Railway Society (*Railway Modeller*, May 1980). Protofour standards took Irish modelling into greater realms of realism, with Tony Miles building at least one GNR(I) locomotive with full working inside valve gear and tender-mounted motor. Interest was not limited to 4mm. Other models of the period included an N gauge Bagenalstown (*Railway Modeller,* February 1980) and Richard Chown's expanding modular Castle Rackrent in 7mm (*Railway Modeller*, March 1975 and February 1978; *Model Railways* May 1975 and August 1978).

The situation is a lot better now, with at least one steam and one diesel locomotive produced by major manufacturers in ready-to-run form. There are also a number of smaller suppliers producing body kits for locomotives, carriages and wagons in a variety of materials such as white metal, etched brass and resin. With more kits and ready to run ready models under development, the future of modelling Irish railways seems bright.

The model railway press has existed since 1925, carrying occasional Irish articles, but in 1992 Ivor Hughes as editor launched *Irish Lines*, building on a small group of enthusiasts drawn together by Jonathan James' enterprise of compiling a comprehensive index of drawings for Irish locomotives and rolling stock. By the summer of 1995, the membership had grown to 30, with Patrick O'Sullivan taking over as editor in November 1995. *Irish Lines* ran for 13 issues, to March 1996, but was relaunched as *New Irish Lines* in the following year. It continues to appear twice yearly, carrying plans, prototype information, construction articles, news from the subscribers and product reviews, and allows those modelling, or just interested in Irish railways, to exchange ideas and information. By tradition, it still describes itself as the newsletter of the Irish Railway Modelling Circle, although such a body has never strictly existed!

Modelling Irish railways is now more popular than ever, stimulated by a number of recent high quality books and the desire to build something more unusual than another GWR branch terminus. The three barriers which have put some people off are the Irish gauge, the lack of commercial support and the dearth of suitable drawings and information. However, as we explain in the following chapters, none of these are insurmountable and we hope that this book will encourage others to have a go at this fascinating and ever so varied subject, just as we have.

Left: **Two further examples of Cyril Fry's original models are seen here, a tram on the Dublin to Dalkey route and by way of contrast, a West Clare Railway 0-6-2 tank engine and one of the line's Tourist Saloons.** Both, Des McGlynn collection

CHAPTER 2

SCALES & GAUGES

If there is one particular area of model railways that causes the most difficulty for the individual, it must be scales and gauges. Many people seem to get the two items confused with each other and introduce the third element of wheel standards. So, the best thing to do is to start from basics and examine each area of this confusing topic in order to make an informed decision on which way to go.

Scale

The word scale is used to describe the size of the model in relation to the real thing. Two measurements are often quoted, but they amount to the same thing. The first measurement is expressed as a ratio, such as 1:76 scale. This simply means that the model is 76 times smaller than the full size prototype. The scale can also be expressed as how many millimetres there are to 1ft of the original size. So, 1:76 scale can also be expressed as 4mm to1ft. The latter measurement is the more usually used, often abbreviated to just the first set of measurements as 4mm scale.

Gauge

The word gauge is used just as it is on the real railway, the measurement of the distance between the running rails, usually expressed in millimetres for modelling.

Popular sizes

By using a combination of particular scales and gauges, we can arrive at some of the popular sizes used for model railways, such as O, OO, HO and N gauge. The scales used are 7mm:1ft, 4mm:1ft, 3.5mm:1ft and 2mm:1ft respectively, whereas the gauges used are 32mm, 16.5mm for both OO and HO, and 9mm. There is a great deal of commercial support for these popular sizes. The choice of which to use is governed by how much room the modeller may have available for a layout and what length of train is run.

Compromise

The astute mathematician will by now have realised that there is a problem with some of the scales and gauges used in the popular sizes. If a scale of 4mm:1ft is used for the British standard gauge of 4ft 8½in then the model track gauge used should be 18.83mm and not 16.5mm as the latter equates to a full size gauge of 4ft 1½in, somewhat narrower than it should be. A similar problem exists with N gauge. The reasons for this compromise are a result of the size of the mechanisms used when these sizes were first introduced many years ago. They have since become the norm and the majority of modellers are willing to accept the compromise. Continental and North American modellers also use 16.5mm track, but use a scale of 3.5mm:1ft, more commonly known as HO Scale. In HO, the track is the correct width for British standard gauge. As there is a certain amount of interchangeability, the size is often referred to as OO/HO gauge. So, where does that put the Irish modeller? Well, we are either going to model broad gauge (the Irish standard gauge) of 5ft 3in or the Irish narrow gauge of 3ft. In the popular scale of 4mm:1ft these would work out as 21mm and 12mm gauge respectively.

Solution – broad gauge

There are a number of acceptable solutions to this problem and we do not need to get too bogged down in it all. The most popular scale used for modelling Irish railways is the 4mm to the foot. Commercially available ready to run stock has been produced by various manufacturers such as Hornby, Lima and Bachmann. All these models run on 16.5mm gauge track. In addition, many smaller manufacturers produce a variety of kits in this scale, some using chassis components provided in the kit and some being designed to use a ready-to-run chassis purchased separately. The common feature is that they all use 16.5mm gauge, or OO gauge track. The advantage with all this is that the modeller need not get into the realms of track and chassis building. There have been a number of layouts built using this principle such as Ballinagee (*Railway Modeller,* April 1986 and October 1995), the co-author's own Dunmore & Fidlin (*Railway Modeller,* December 1996) and Brian McCann's Ballyowen (*Railway Modeller*, January 2002). The results are quite acceptable and enable the modeller to get up and running fairly quickly with reliable results.

The same compromise is made in 2mm scale, although here, the error is less noticeable because of the overall smaller size. The track should be 10.5mm gauge, just 1.5mm wider than the commercially available N gauge track of 9mm. As with OO gauge, many of the N gauge chassis can be used, but there is little available in the way of suitable bodies. However, Bagenalstown (*Railway Modeller*, February 1980), shows what can be achieved. Modellers using 7mm:1ft can use O gauge track, which is 32mm wide. The correct width should be 36.75mm. There are a number of commercially available chassis and kits to support 7mm scale and a number of layouts have used this size, such as Richard Chown's Castle Rackrent (*Railway Modeller*, March 1975).

Solution – narrow gauge

The solution for the narrow gauge modeller is somewhat easier. In 4mm scale, the track gauge for 3ft gauge works out as exactly 12mm. This is the gauge used by the old Tri-ang TT system and continental HOm narrow gauge railways. Although there are a few continental ready to run models on the market, Tri-ang TT track and models have not been produced for some years. A few kits make use of various chassis produced for these systems. It must be said though, that searching for various Tri-ang TT gauge chassis can be time consuming. However, a lot of the kits do come with a complete chassis (see Chapter 6 for more on the narrow gauge).

Alternatives

As always, there are a number of alternative combinations that can be used. Modellers of the Irish narrow gauge are quite well catered for in this respect. One such combination is to use 16.5mm track and mechanisms with a scale of 5.5mm:1ft. There are some kits available for this size and it can be quite effectively used as can be seen with John Seward's model of Inver on the County Donegal network (*Railway Modeller*, August and September 1999). Another combination is to use N gauge track and mechanisms with a scale of 3mm:1ft. Again, there are some kits available and Charles Insley's Cahir Patrick (*Railway Modeller*, June 2003) shows just what can be done in this scale.

Broad gauge modellers run into a few more difficulties here, if they wish to use an exact scale–gauge ratio for 5ft 3in. In almost every case, it means the modeller has to build the trackwork and modify or build the chassis. This is not quite as daunting as it may first appear. There are a number of suppliers who produce parts for track building. These parts include rails, sleepers, templates, jigs and gauges. In the popular 7mm, 4mm and 2mm scales, many of the commercially produced chassis can be modified for use on the wider track. In 4mm scale there are a couple of ways of tackling this. The 4mm scale EM gauge uses a track width of 18.2mm and wheels of a finer profile than commercial OO. Although 18.2mm is still too narrow, the overall appearance is improved and track is commercially available from specialist suppliers. The ultimate in 4mm scale is to use 21mm gauge, the exact scale width for 5ft 3in. Now, this gauge can be used to OO, EM or P4 standards, so what's the difference? The difference in these three standards is based on the tolerances used for the wheels and track, OO being the most coarse and P4 being the finest. Many modellers who choose to model with 21mm gauge track use P4 standards. There is good commercial support for this standard and it really isn't as difficult as it may first appear, but it does require a lot of time consuming work on behalf of the modeller. The results, however, can be impressive as can be seen with Adavoyle (*Railway Modeller*, May 1980). We will return to finescale modelling on such exact scale-gauge combinations as 21mm gauge in 4mm scale in Chapter 7.

GAUGE/SCALE COMBINATIONS USED FOR MODELLING IRISH RAILWAYS

This table shows the various scale and gauge combinations which modellers have used or proposed over the years for Irish prototypes.,

SCALE	GAUGE	REMARKS
15mm:1ft.	45mm	Used for 3ft lines on garden layouts: LGB and similar chassis and mechanisms can be adapted
14mm / 15mm /16mm: 1ft.	32mm	Used for 3ft lines on garden layouts: strictly too narrow, but mixes with 16mm:1ft. (widely used for 2ft prototypes). Several steam and at least one diesel locomotive have been manufactured.
10mm:1ft.	32mm	Limited commercial support for 3ft prototypes
7mm:1ft.	36.75mm	Correct gauge / scale ratio for 5ft 3in
7mm:1ft.	32mm	Broad gauge models, running on 'too narrow' 0 gauge track
7mm:1ft.	21mm	Correct gauge / scale ratio for 3ft: some kits available, and now suitable axles for re-gauging commercial wheels
6mm:1ft.	32mm	Near correct gauge / scale ratio for 5ft 3in on 0 gauge track
5.5mm:1ft.	16.5mm	3ft gauge models, using commercial 00 mechanisms and wheels: a few kits available
3/16in.:1ft.	63/64in.	Correct gauge / scale ratio for 5ft 3in in S-scale
4mm:1ft.	16.5 mm	Broad gauge models, running on 'too narrow' 00 gauge track. Most kits designed to suit 16.5, 18 or 21mm gauge
4mm:1ft.	18mm	Broad gauge models, running on 'too narrow' EM gauge track
4mm:1ft.	21mm	Correct gauge / scale ratio for 5ft 3in
4mm:1ft. gauge	12mm	For 3ft gauge lines, good range of kits, mostly also suitable for 9mm which is more popular for narrow gauge in 4mm scale
3.5mm:1ft.	18mm	Near correct scale ratio for 5ft 3in using HO scale on EM gauge
3mm:1ft.	16.5mm	Theoretical combination: actually 3 scale inches too wide, but would allow use of 00 track, wheels and some mechanisms
101.6:1	15.75mm	Correct ratio for 5ft 3in in 3mm fine scale. TT3b 5ft 3in in 3mm Society nomenclature
3mm:1ft.	9mm	3ft lines: some kits
2 1/16mm	9mm	Broad gauge models, running on 'too narrow' N gauge track
2mm:1ft.	10.5mm	Correct gauge/scale ratio for 5ft 3in in 2mm finescale
2mm:1ft.	6.5mm	Nn3 scale: approximately 3ft narrow gauge, using Z gauge track and chassis: at least one Bord na Móna railcar model built so far!

Conclusion

There is a bewildering variety of different scales, gauges and standards that can be used for Irish modelling. The choice depends on a number of factors and can be summarised as follows:

1) Decide whether you want to model broad gauge or narrow gauge.

2) Decide how long your trains are going to be (full length main line trains or short branch line sets) and work out the room you require for a given scale. Full length trains can be quite big, up to 10ft for a 4mm scale 10 coach train!

3) According to the space at your disposal, choose a suitable scale.

4) In the scale you have chosen, use the nearest commercially supported 4ft 8½in gauge track and ignore the difference. A number of attractive OO and N gauge layouts have been built this way.

5) Alternatively, use a recognised scale such as 7mm, 4mm or 2mm, but build your own track and chassis to the correct Irish gauge (36.75mm, 21mm or 10.5mm respectively). This allows the use of a wide range of accessories made for the British market. This way, you get the impressive 'broad gauge look', but it is time consuming.

6) Choose a commercially supported gauge, but modify your scale to get the correct ratio. The advantage here is that you have access to wheels, axles and track components and possibly some ready to run mechanisms.

Thus the modeller has a number of options. Which one you choose will depend on what you want to achieve, how much work you want to put in and your particular level of skill. The main point is that you should pick an option that suits you and that you can gain maximum enjoyment from.

Right: **A GNR(I) cattle wagon built from a white metal kit made by the Model Wagon Company. This 4mm scale model has been built for OO gauge 16.5mm track.** Stephen Johnson

Below: **A finescale model of the Sligo, Leitrim & Northern Counties 0-6-4 tank locomotive *Lissadell*, in 7mm scale. This model was built by Adrian Rowland from one of his own kits.** Adrian Rowland

Bottom: **The distinctive polychrome brick construction, which was used by the GNR for many buildings across its system, is exactly replicated on Tony Miles' magnificent Adavoyle Junction layout. The track is handbuilt to 21mm gauge using P4 standards. GNR 'S' class 4-4-0 *Lugnaquilla* stands at the platform.** Tony Wright, courtesy British Railway Modelling

Top: **'SG3' class 0-6-0 No 97 passes Knockmore Junction signal cabin with a mixed goods. Harry Mulholland's 7mm layout is based on the three way junction south of Lisburn on the GNR main line where the routes to Antrim and Banbridge left the Belfast to Dublin line.**

Above: **One interesting feature of Adavoyle Junction is that part of the layout where Ireland's two gauges are seen side by side. The difference between them is nicely illustrated in this view, as GNR railbus F3 on the 5ft 3in gauge passes the Tralee & Dingle Railway Hunslet built 2-6-0T No 2 on a narrow gauge goods train.** Both, Tony Wright, courtesy British Railway Modelling

Left: **An advantage of using 4mm scale 16.5mm track is that one can use ready-to-run chassis with little modification. This resin bodied kit of an IÉ '201' class runs on an Athearn SD45 chassis. Here, No 210 *River Erne* stands in the bay at Dunmore & Fidlin.** Stephen Johnson

CHAPTER 3

MODELLING THE BROAD GAUGE

For anyone wanting to model British railway practice, at least in the more popular scales of OO and N, a trip to a decent model shop, or a browse through the mail order section of one of the current magazines will provide access to ready-to-run locomotives, rolling stock and track. Assuming basic carpentry skills and the ability to assemble buildings and such accessories from card and plastic kits, in a few weeks the aspiring modeller can have an attractive layout. True, such models appeared in the *Model Railway News* up to 70 years ago, but then, when most proprietary items were crude toys, and the trade supplied only such basic components as lengths of rail and wheels, each layout represented many months of toil and a high degree of skill in soldering, shaping and cutting. Finescale models, made to order, were then available at prices that seem unbelievable, until one reckons for inflation, and realises that each represented a good week's wage in the 1930s. In terms of looks and performance, the models now on the shelves of your local shop will probably exceed these. Hand-built models are still an option, and they will always have an edge on mass-produced items, but at a price of five to ten times the proprietary ones.

Until recently, anyone intending to model Irish railways was back in the 1930s situation. Assuming he chose a scale supported by the trade like 4mm, there were basic components, such as castings, turnings and track parts, but each locomotive and coach had to be assembled from these and raw materials like brass or Plasticard. Although a few train sets were 'customised' for the Irish market, such as a Hornby Hymek in CIÉ livery, a Lima Class 33 masquerading as an 'A' class or a freelance 0-4-0T in green with the CIÉ 'flying snail' logo, there were no serious models.

More dedicated commercial support for the Irish scene began 25 years ago. Model Irish Railways (MIR) was formed in 1979 to produce accurate models of modern Irish prototypes, and since then followers of the contemporary scene have benefited from their range of kits for locomotives and wagons, paints and transfers. At about the same time, Modern Traction Kits (MTK) introduced Irish locomotive, coach and railcar kits and more recently some of these kits have been upgraded and reissued by No-nonsense Kits. In 1980, TMD Models (later Studio Scale Models) produced an etched brass kit for the MGWR 'E' class 0-6-0T. Q Kits appeared at the same time offering white-metal kits and resin bodies of CIÉ diesels such as the 'A' and 'C' classes.

Over the years a small, but steadily growing, number of such kits have appeared. Although quicker than scratch-building, they do require a fair degree of skill in handling metal components. Now, two reasonably accurate Irish locomotives, one steam, one diesel, are available to run on OO track, and some rolling stock, but what does the modeller who is not confident about scratch-building or tackling etched brass do, if a proper working layout is required, rather than something to sit in a display case? To some extent, the solution depends on how you have tackled the gauge problem (see Chapter 2). If you are going to use 'correct gauge' (such as 21mm in 4mm scale), and work to finescale, you will almost certainly want to hand build your models to high degrees of accuracy, although today a few commercial models may be good enough to re-gauge.

But, if you have decided to compromise on a popular gauge, such as OO, it is not as clear-cut. In some ways, you will be in the situation faced by OO modellers in the 1960s. A few accurate models were then available, chiefly for the English Great Western Railway, but fans of other lines developed quite an eye for conversion jobs, adapting the commercial models on the market to produce a wider range of locomotives and stock.

The Irish enthusiast is aided by the fact that in the 19th century, the Irish Sea was neither a political nor a geographical barrier, and many professional engineers moved freely across it, as part of their training and career. So, Irish locomotive and rolling stock practice often assumed that 'familiar but different' feel for observers from across the water: the British connection was clear, but often with a Celtic flair. The most obvious case was the Belfast & Northern Counties Railway, where after 1903 as the NCC, a division of the English Midland Railway, mechanical practice acquired a decidedly Derby style. The rest of this chapter describes some of the various 'conversions' modellers have used over the years to produce 'something Irish' from British outline models. As with the gauge issue, this is of course a compro-

Right: **One of the easiest conversions to provide an Irish locomotive is one of the NCC 'Y' class 0-6-0Ts, from the Tri-ang (now Hornby) LMS 'Jinty'. In OO, only minor changes to the body are needed. This example runs on EM gauge, so it has a new chassis.** Alan O'Rourke

mise: you may produce a model that captures the flavour and feel of an Irish locomotive or coach, and is instantly recognisable as such, but unless you go to the bother of tracking down proper drawings and making it yourself to these, it will not be an accurate model. That does not of course prevent you deriving considerable pleasure from making and running it. If you are quite new to model railways, it is best to serve a sort of 'apprenticeship'. Start with some simple re-paints, and maybe minor cosmetic changes to the superstructure, leaving the mechanism well alone! As you gain in confidence, go for more major surgery, or maybe tackle a body kit, or even build your own superstructures to go on a commercial chassis. Maybe then you will feel happy at constructing a white metal wagon kit such as those from the MIR range and move on to scratch-built wagons or perhaps etched brass kits. Remember that for 'carving up' it is better to try and get second hand items from one of the swap-meets than buying nice new boxed models.

OO gauge locomotives

Because of the LMS connection, there are several possible NCC conversions from commercial models. The easiest is the Hornby LMS '3F' 'Jinty' 0-6-0T. The LMS re-gauged two of these and sent them over to Belfast in 1944. They became the NCC's 'Y' class and were mostly used for shunting. The ready-to-run model just requires repainting and a few minor detail changes, which are clear from studying the published photographs of the Irish engines. Similarly, the Hornby or Dapol '2P' is close to a 'U2'. The 'WT' class, or 'Jeep', in theory should be an easy conversion, but in practice the footplate causes problems. Modellers have adapted both the Wrenn (formerly Hornby Dublo) and the Hornby Fowler 2-6-4T. One supplier has promised an accurate ready-to-run model of this class, but delivery is now way overdue.

To build an LMS/NCC 'WT' class from the Dublo/Wrenn 2-6-4T, remove the body from the chassis and cut away the sloping footplate just ahead of the cylinders. Raise the top of the dome to the same height as the chimney with filler. File off the smokebox number plate and handle and replace the latter with a central wheel. Use Plasticard or something similar to make the topfeed fitting for the boiler. The front of the cab needs building up to remove the swept back appearance, and the door openings to the cab need some re-modelling. If starting from the Hornby Fowler model, cut off the front vertical face of the footplate ahead of the cylinders. Further trim the footplate ahead of the tanks to a shell, and along the bottom line of the tanks to give the double step. Cut off and re-site the front footplate, filing about 1mm off the buffer beam which is too deep. As with the other model, remove the smokebox handle and replace with the wheel which was a feature of many Irish locomotives. The pipework and handrails on either side of the smokebox also need attention. Add Plasticard footsteps to the tank fronts, and re-site the mushroom vents on the tanks further back, with new tool brackets on the right hand tank. Add boiler topfeed as for the Wrenn model. The firebox needs shortening by 2-3mm and the bunker sides lowering, but be careful as this part of the body includes one of the screws that attaches the chassis to the body. The cab and bunker also need remodelling in Plasticard or brass sheet.

The Lima 'Crab' may, with some fairly hefty modifications to the front end, undergo metamorphosis into a 'W' class Mogul. A new cab, footplate, and deeper buffer beams are needed, and a better match for the boiler fittings can be made by using Fowler pattern ones from the Alan Gibson range. The tender also needs widening. and, as it has tender drive, depending on your choice of gauge and track standards, the mechanism may also need attention.

The Great Northern Railway is not as easy as the NCC. At least two modellers have converted the Hornby 'Schools' into a 'V' class 4-4-0: the main strength is the nicely detailed outside valve gear. This is, as with most conversions, a compromise, and you will have to settle for a coupled wheelbase 8in too short.

Some ideas for other possible conversions are listed below;

- Dapol LMS '4F to 'SG' or 'SG3' 0-6-0
- Tri-ang 'L1' to 'S' class 4-4-0
- Airfix Dean Goods to 'PG' class 0-6-0
- Tri-ang '3F' to 'UG' class 0-6-0 (the basis of this conversion is the old 0-6-0 tender model, which has only been available second hand for some years, not the 'Jinty' tank which is still in production)
- Hobbytrain of Innsbruck make a German railways 'V65' 0-8-0 diesel, very close to the MAK engine supplied to the GNRB just before its dissolution, although the model is of course HO gauge (i.e. 3.5mm to the foot scale).
- GSR '500' class on the Mainline 'Manor' chassis
- 'J26' 0-6-0T from a heavily rebuilt Mainline LNER 'J72'
- The Airfix GWR Prairie chassis for a CBSCR 4-6-0T
- The Dapol LNER 'N2' class to the GSR '670' class 0-6-2T for the Dublin suburban services
- The Tri-ang 'L1' to GSWR 'D2'
- The Tri-ang '3F' 0-6-0 chassis for ex-DSER 'J8', and possibly other 0-6-0s

Two kits from the GEM LNWR range have Irish applications:

- The 0-6-0ST is close to the six locomotives built at Crewe for the Dundalk, Newry & Greenore line.
- The DSER bought six of the 2-4-2Ts in 1902 and re-gauged them for its suburban services. All but one were repatriated during the locomotive shortage in World War 1, the odd one out lasting until 1936 as GSR 'F3' class number 427.

Left: **Seen in the drab GSR grey livery, is 'J8' class 0-6-0 No 446 (ex-DSER). This is a 4mm scale model, built largely of Plasticard, with turned brass boiler fittings on an adapted Hornby-Tri-ang 0-6-0 chassis, running on EM gauge.**
Alan O'Rourke

Right: **This model of SLNCR six-wheel Saloon brake third No 4, in 7mm scale, was built from an Alphagraphix card body kit, with commercial cast buffers and axle guards and Slaters wheels.** Roger Crombleholme

Below right: **This EM gauge model of GSR (ex-GSWR) six-wheeled Luggage composite No 520, was built largely from Ratio components including spliced side mouldings from their Midland Railway 48ft suburban coaches and running gear from their GWR four-wheelers.** Alan O'Rourke

The diesel era is perhaps a little better catered for than the steam. Lima has produced a ready-to-run General Motors '201' class in IÉ, NIR and Enterprise liveries. Most main line classes are covered by various kits produced by Model Irish Railways and Q Kits. These cover CIÉ's 'A', '071', 'B121', 'B141', 'B181' and '201' classes. The NIR fleet is represented by a '111' and '208' class, shortly to be joined by a Hunslet '101' class. A fairly straightforward shortening of the 'A' class kit will produce either a CIÉ 'C' class or NIR '104' class. With a little surgery, a passable model of the CIÉ 'D' class 0-6-0 diesel-electric shunter can be made from the Lima or Bachmann Class 08. Q Kits used to make a resin body for the 'E' class and you might be lucky to find one of these second hand. The little 'G' class can be made two ways. One is from the Worsley Works etched brass kit of the 'G611' type. The other is from a Fleischmann, Orenstein & Koppel 'BRMV9' class body, modified and mounted on a Tenshodo 24.5mm wheelbase motor bogie. The body is centre cab design, so you need to cut off the bonnet without exhaust pipes and fit a new cab rear sheet, re-profile some of the windows and fit new buffer beams, front step handrails and marker lights. As already mentioned, Hobbytrain of Innsbruck make a German 'V65' 0-8-0 diesel, very close to the MAK engine supplied to the GNR Board which later became the sole CIÉ 'K' class locomotive. Just for completeness, Worsley Works produce an etched brass body kit of the 'F' class 3ft gauge diesel locomotives which were used on the West Clare section of CIÉ. Suitable chassis for these diesel kits come from various sources, such as the Airfix/Lima Class 31 for an 'A' class and the Athearn 'SD9s' for the '071/111' class, although at least one modeller has shortened the SD9 to fit in an 'A' class. The Athearn 'SD45' is used under the '201' class whilst the Athearn 'SW1500' can be used with the 'B121' class. The Airfix and Athearn chassis are easily converted to 21mm gauge P4 standards. The diesel scene looks to improve further with plans for a better quality 'A' class body kit in resin and a ready-to-run 'B141/B181' class from Bachmann. The correct shade paints are available from Model Irish Railways and Precision Paints. Transfers, number sets, lining and even the tricky to paint 'speed whiskers' are also available.

Two rather unusual small industrial prototypes can be modelled using the Tenshodo motor bogie. This can easily be converted to 21mm gauge by fitting new 1.5mm silver steel axles. These locomotives are the Irish shell 'Planet' diesel, which is preserved at Whitehead by the Railway Preservation Society of Ireland. A body kit can be obtained from Nonneminstre Models. Also, one of the Ruston 88DS shunters, used at sugar beet refineries in the Irish Republic can also be created, using a body kit from Impetus Models.

OO gauge coaches, railcars and multiple units

For some modellers, the engine is, as Drew Donaldson would have said, 'the heart and soul' of the layout. Rolling stock has never attracted as much attention from observers or photographers as what was pulling it, and for some modellers the rest of the train, as long as the vehicles are roughly the right size and colour, is immaterial. But, for some enthusiasts, building accurate coaches and wagons is at least as fascinating as getting the engine right. In historical terms, the passenger coach has undergone a process of design divergence followed by convergence. The earliest carriages, such as those used on the D&K, were clearly derived from contemporary horse-drawn road vehicles. While third class passengers were lucky to have anything better than an open wagon, their 'betters' travelled in vehicles clearly based on three stage coach bodies, joined on a short chassis fitted with flanged wheels, a chain coupling and horsehair-stuffed buffers. The stage coach origin was clearly reflected in the hinged doors on both sides of each compartment, the quarter round windows and the curved body sides, common to the vehicles of most early lines.

By the 1870s, although most companies continued to turn out four-wheelers for local services, main line coaches ran on six wheels, and were up to about 34ft long. The extra set of wheels supposedly gave better riding, certainly in the middle of the vehicle, but those in the end compartments still got bounced around. By now, most companies had established their own distinctive combinations of body profile (including the 'tumblehome' bringing the wider body into the narrower chassis), roof contour, external decorative square or round corner panelling or beading, and fittings like door and grab handles. Such distinctive designs, with which the various companies embellished their vehicles, are not easy to model. From the 1880s, Irish companies introduced bogie coaches, starting at about 45ft long, and with the same body styles as the six-wheelers. By now, some vehicle had lavatories and short internal corridors, but such luxuries were usually for the better elements of society, and Third class passengers, packed six a side in their compartments, often on bare boards, had to hold on for the next station stop. The MGWR was the exception among the larger Irish lines and it built no bogie coaches until the very end of the 19th century. By then, main line coaches were leaping forward in comfort and design, with the addition of features such as steam heating, electric lighting and end gangway connections. For most Irish and British companies, the classic main line coach evolved in the Edwardian period, 50 to 60ft long, with an elliptical roof for more headroom, and a series of compartments, linked on one side by a corridor with three or four hinged external doors. On the opposite side, each compartment still had the traditional drop-light door, flanked by two quarter-light windows. Lavatories were provided for all classes at one or both ends. In the 1930s, the design was slightly modernised, with flush steel panels replacing the ornately panelled wooden body-work. The design and style of the windows on the 'compartment' side was re-modelled to provide one large picture window to each compartment. Entrance and exit was through two or three doors whilst some vehicles now had central vestibules. This body plan lasted until the move to open saloon type coaches after World War 2, with seats in bays of fours or sixes on either side of a central aisle.

Going back to the older vehicles, the main problem for modellers is the ornate body panelling. Until the 1960s, most ready-to-run British models were based on the British Railways Mark I coach, sometimes rather under scale length. These were sold in a variety of regional or pre-nationalisation liveries. However, when Tri-ang produced two unusual locomotives, from the pre-World War 1 era, they required coaches from an earlier period. For the GWR *Lord of the Isles* Single, the company produced two types of compartment coaches with clerestory roofs, a bit short, but approximating to some of William Dean's early stock for the GWR.

Modellers rapidly saw the potential of the fully panelled moulded plastic bodies for splicing, cutting and joining in various combinations, to produce vehicles from the London & South Western, South Eastern & Chatham and many other pre-grouping railways. The Tri-ang clerestory body style is quite close to the GSWR 45-50ft non-corridor bogie coaches built in 1885-1910. Since then, Ratio have produced a series of 48ft panelled Midland Railway suburban coaches, which can also be cut and joined to make models of GSWR 30ft six-wheelers and arc-roofed non-corridor bogie stock. The Ratio range also includes GWR four wheelers, and the 30ft Brake third has almost exactly the same panelling as some two-compartment Brake thirds built in the 1890s for the WLWR. The sides from the Ratio kits are available from the makers, which is more economical for 'kit-bashers' than buying boxed kits. The two 28ft Ratio GWR four-wheelers, a five compartment Third and a four compartment Composite, are also similar to some of the DSER's six-wheel suburban coaches. A few other GSWR 30ft designs can be produced by lengthening the sides from kits previously made by K's for London, Brighton & South Coast Railway four-wheelers with duckets and double doors left over from Ratio or Tri-ang conversions. However, since these kits were entirely cast in white metal, they can be a bit top-heavy. The main problem with most of this is making a working six-wheel chassis, and for those not feeling like building their own there are two options: the compensated kits from Brassmasters, or the radial chassis used by Hornby for their six-wheel sausage vans.

For anyone wanting more accurate models Worsley Works have produced some basic kits whilst Studio Scale Models have produced complete etched brass kits for several of these six wheeled vehicles. The six-wheelers also included some full Brakes.

The second Tri-ang old time locomotive was the Caledonian Railway Neilson 4-2-2 No 123, and to go with this there were Composite and Brake coaches based on that railway's 12-wheel Grampian coaches. Here, there was even more compromise than for the GWR clerestories, as the coaches, though of scale length, used the four-wheel bogies, roof, chassis and end mouldings of BR Mark I models. The sides however were quite well detailed and the panelling was typical of the Edwardian period side corridor compartment stock, with one external door to each compartment on the non-corridor side. These coaches like the clerestories appeared in a variety of liveries over the years, but never attracted the same attention from 'kit-bashers'. The body style however is quite close to GSWR/GSR 57ft vehicles of the 1915-1928 period, and may also be adaptable to MGWR panelled vehicles of the same era. The early period panelled LMS stock made by Mainline is also quite close to this GSWR /GSR design of coach.

Transport Research Associates of Dublin produced a drawing book of all GSWR coaches as running at the time of the 1925 amalgamation some years ago, including the surviving stock from the WLWR, Waterford & Central Ireland Railway and Waterford & Wexford Railway. The drawings came out at slightly larger than 4mm scale in some cases, but were very useful for modelling . Sadly, this work is long out of print, but copies do sometimes come up on the second hand market, and the full bibliographic details are: Richards H, Pender B (1974) *GSWR Carriage Diagrams Dublin*: Transport Research Associates.

Opposite page bottom: **This CIÉ (ex-GSWR/GSR) bogie Composite in OO gauge was created from a Hornby model of a GWR Corridor Composite.** Peter Swift

Top right: **This 4mm model of a GSR six-wheel Third brake, which originated on the WLWR, was built largely from Ratio components, including the sides from the GWR four-wheel Brake third kit.** Alan O'Rourke

Below: **An OO gauge model of CIÉ (ex-GSR) Bredin designed Third No 1335 was built from the Hornby LMS Composite, lengthened with an extra door vestibule from a BR Mark I vehicle.**

Below centre: **CIÉ (ex-GSWR) clerestory roofed Brake composite No 861 was modelled in OO gauge from the Hornby GWR clerestory Composite or Third. The original model needed to be lengthened to allow for the van part of the vehicle and it also had to be fitted with six wheel bogies.** Both, Peter Swift

Prototype	Model	Adaptations/Notes
GSWR 57ft corridor third	Graham Farish corridor	You can either use the original vehicle for the elliptical roofed Composite coaches, or re-profile the ends and fit a new roof for the arc roofed prototypes. Some alterations to the windows on the corridor side, louvres, and chassis required.
GSWR 12-wheel clerestory Brake Composite	Hornby GWR clerestory	Needs a Plasticard extension to the body to make the van portion and alterations to some of the windows. The original bogies need to be replaced by six-wheeled bogies set at 172mm pivot centres. Westward GWR pattern bogies are the closest match.
GSR Pullman	Hornby	The GSR owned four of these, fairly similar to the current Hornby model, which provides the characteristic bogies, roof profile and end vestibules. The main difference for the Irish vehicle is the match-boarding rather than flush panelling below the waist. To be more correct, the windows will also need re-arranging on one side. It is also possible to splice pairs of older Tri-ang Pullmans, which were under scale length.
GSWR/GSR Corridor Composite of the 1920s period	Hornby GWR Corridor Composite	Lengthened with Plasticard and with some alterations to the windows and underframe.
GSR 60ft steel panelled stock	Airfix LMS Composite	This model is the correct length and has a similar body profile to Bredin's Composites and Thirds. Some of the Irish vehicles also had centre vestibules and lavatories. Similar vehicles were built by CIÉ, some on Bulleid underframes. The Hornby LMS Composite, is too short to make a GSR coach, but can be spliced and lengthened with a suitable spare vestibule section, and alterations to windows, underframe and roof. Studio Scale Models supply kits of both the Third class and First/Third Composite. The kits require wheels, bearings, seating and paint. Worsley Works also produce a kit for a 1937 First corridor.
CIÉ Bulleid 'laminate' stock (1145, 1356, 1429 and 1449 series)	Hornby Stanier 57ft coaches Airfix or Dapol 60ft LMS Composites	Some types can be adapted from the Hornby Mk II Open second, by removing the centre vestibule and shortening the body. For some vehicles you will needs new ends to produce the characteristic taper to the body sides, re-modelling of the windows and alterations to the roof vents. The main problem is the distinctive Bulleid triangulated underframe. The best option may be a spare BR Mark I underframe, with Commonwealth bogies and 12mm wheels, or the Bachmann BR ones, with smaller wheels, and a new external equalising beam added. Worsley Works produce kits for a Standard open and a Brake standard open.
Bulleid four-wheel 'tin vans'		Scratch-built Plasticard or brass body on Parkside LMS CCT kit underframe.
CIÉ Park Royal coaches	Hornby Stanier 57ft coaches	These 57ft coaches can be adapted by removing the door and toilet windows from each end of the same vehicle and replacing with flat sided plasticard extensions, to bring the vehicle up to prototype 61ft 6in length, over headstocks. The chassis and roof will also need splicing and lengthening. Worsley Works also produce a 'scratch aid' body and underframe etch. There is a reasonable amount of work required to complete a carriage and the modeller will have to supply their own bogies, interiors and roof. However, the etched sides do make construction of one of these distinctive carriages a lot easier.
Cravens coaches	Lima Mk IIb	Worsley Works supply an etched body and underframe for the Cravens carriage as part of their 'scratch aid' range. The modeller will have to provide suitable bogies (BR B4 type), interiors and roof.
LMS/NCC coaches MR/LMS type D1700 diagram, LMS period I design NCC Nos, 171-6; 190-3; 198, 199 NCC diagram J11		To deal with extra wartime traffic and to replace vehicles destroyed at York Road station in the Blitz, the LMS sent second hand coaches (some of which were built before the British grouping in 1923 by the Midland Railway) to the NCC 1941-2. In some cases these can be made from kits for the original LMS/MR designs. Use sides from Comet Models and other parts from the Jackson Evans range.

Prototype	Model	Adaptations/Notes
D1784 diagram, LMS period II design, Nos 177-82		Parts from Jackson Evans range, sides from Comet Models
D1906 diagram, LMS period III design, Nos 183-4 and 194-7	Perseverance Models	Sides from Comet Models
D1281 64, 65, 68, 69 F3		Etches from Alan Gibson*
D1282 230; 234;236;238; 241;242 J12		Etches from Alan Gibson*

* Brass overlays for the Bachman ready-to-run coaches. May only be available as part of a set of etches for six coaches, two each of these and two other vehicles, which were not represented in Ireland. Now marketed by: David Geen, 30 Silverwood Close, Dale Park, Hartlepool, Cleveland TN27 3QF.

For later NCC coaches, use the LMS 9ft wheelbase riveted bogies; for earlier BNCR vehicles the GNR (England)/LNER 8ft Fox pattern bogies are a good match. At the time of writing, MJT sell castings for both these bogie patterns.

Turning to the GNR(I), the Dapol 60ft Stanier coach has also been used as the basis of the GNR(I) F16 coaches and the Mainline BR Mark I Composite can be adapted for the C2 side corridor, six compartment all First, Studio Scale Models make etched brass kits for the K15 Third and L12 Brake third, both examples of the later steel panelled flush-sided coaches, and they also make castings for bogies and other GNR(I) coach fittings. Worsley Works have recently produced a range of etched sides for the following GNR(I) coaches:

Class	Type	Other Details
B9	Buffet car	58ft flush sided
F16	First/Third Composite corridor	58ft flush sided
I13	Tri-composite	58ft panelled
J4	Tri-composite brake	58ft panelled
K8	Third class open	58ft panelled
K11	Third class open	58ft panelled
K13	3rd Class Corridor	58ft panelled
K15	Third open	58ft panelled
L9	Third brake	58ft panelled
L10	3rd brake	58ft panelled
L12	3 compartment Third brake	58ft flush sided
L13	Third brake	58ft flush sided

As with the NCC, the GNR(I) resorted to the expediency of second hand stock from the LMS, in this case buying 18 vehicles of LNWR origin, in 1948.Two of these can be produced from commercial kits:

LNWR type	GNR(I) number	GNR type	Model
D268 arc roof	475	Corridor third	Ratio plastic kit.
D133 elliptical roof	484	Composite	Sides from the Jackson Evans range.

In the 1930s the main Irish systems went over to steel panelled stock for new construction. The NCC vehicles were of course to LMS patterns, and so are close to the commercial models made for that line, but the GSR carriages designed by Bredin were very similar and GSR and NCC stock can be modelled by slicing and lengthening Mainline LMS coaches, or directly from Hornby Stanier 57ft coaches. The table on pages 18 and 19 shows ways in which examples of GSWR, GSR, CIÉ, LMS/NCC and GNR bogie coaching stock can be recreated from other model coaches which are on the market.

In the years following World War 2, CIÉ, the UTA and the GNR(I) all ordered diesel railcars. Some of these can be created by converting other models. For example:

- CIÉ AEC and ex-GNR(I) railcar sets from the Tri-ang DMU.
- GNR(I)/UTA 4-car 'BUT' set: dummy power cars from much modified Airfix Mk IIs, and the trailers from Hornby and Mainline products.
- MPDs: from Hornby LMS Stanier 57ft coaches, two Composites and a Brake third, the later fitted with a motor bogie from the same maker's Hymek, with added plasticard cabs.
- MEDs: from Dapol 60ft coaches, using the modified chassis from the Hornby DMU centre car, and a motor bogie; that from the Hymek seems the most suitable.

In recent years, the use of airline-type seats for mainline stock has become popular, while even on suburban trains the traditional compartment arrangement has been replaced by open seating. Particularly in Ireland of course, new stock was largely built for the expresses, and passengers on local and branch trains had to make do with older designs. In Ireland until the 1960s that sometimes meant a six-wheeler! In the last 30 years, coach design has converged again, and most locomotive hauled stock supplied to both Irish systems since the 1970s has been to British Rail Mark II and Mark III designs, some in fact being second hand BR vehicles on re-gauged bogies.

There are various ways to produce a rake of modern stock. In recent years, Lima and Model Irish Railways have produced a number of repainted Mark IIFs and Mark IIIAs in various liveries. The notable exceptions are those obligatory and curious features of CIÉ/IÉ passenger train formations, the steam heating van (GSV) and the electric generating van (EGV). Right from the start of dieselisation, CIÉ decided not to clutter up its diesel locomotives with boilers or generators. Instead, these became the responsibility of the guard and were placed in a modified brake van. However, the situation changed with the introduction of the '201' class and Enterprise De Dietrich carriages. On these sets the '201' class do provide power (head end power) for carriage heating and ventilation and these sets to not include an EGV in the rake.For those modelling CIÉ, a variety of transfers, lining and made-up number sets are available from Model Irish Railways. The correct shade golden-brown paint is also available from Model Irish Railways or Precision Paints.

IÉ purchased 16 second hand Mark IIA/B/C carriages from BR in 1990 in an effort to replace all the remaining wooden bodied and laminate carriages from the fleet on safety grounds. Both Hornby and Lima make versions of these carriages and a simple repaint should suffice. The last of the prototypes for these vehicles have just been withdrawn from service.

Airfix, GMR, Mainline, and Dapol Mark IIDs and Lima Mark IIFs are similar to CIÉ AC stock. The bodies of the Open first and Open second are close to CIÉ Super-standard and Standard coaches, but require modified underframes, the main difference being the air conditioning units. The Composite can be made by splicing the Second class section from the Brake second onto an Airfix First and the Kitchen second by blocking up some windows on a Second, moving the doors at the kitchen end and adding roof details.

Lima and Jouef Mk IIIA models provide potential conversions to CIÉ Mark IIIs or the Mark III push-pull sets. These are preferred to the Hornby version of these carriages as their older Mark IIIs are too short, having one complete seating bay missing! The Lima Mark IIIs are easier to repaint than the Jouef version, the reason being that the 'flush glazed' appearance of the Jouef coach is achieved by painting the transparent carriage side. To repaint the carriage involves a lot of masking up of the windows.

The AC 5601 series electric generating vans (EGVs) can be made from the Lima (or Airfix/Dapol) Mark II stock (FO, SO or BSO). Strip down the model to the body shell, file the window frames flush, remove the door hinges from carriage ends, the raised roof section over the toilet and the vestibule ventilators. You will need a drawing or good photographs to mark out the windows in the prototype on thin (0.010in) Plasticard to make new overlays, cutting out the window openings, scribing the door lines and then cutting through to make a series of sections from the overlay. Cut slightly oversize window openings in the original body shell to allow you to fit almost flush glazing from an acetate sheet after painting. The overlay is applied in sections, using a suitable glue (such as cyanacryalite adhesive), starting with a little glue at the top to secure each section tight up to the cantrail and then applying more glue and rolling the Plasticard down over the coach tumblehome. Leave a small gap between the panels, allowing the addition of door hinges from microstrip later. New grilles can be added using BR Class 37 nose grilles, made by Howes Models. The roof needs Plasticard rectangles to represent the access hatches (with lifting eyes made from fine wire) and grilles and suitable vents available in the MTK range. Also on the roof, but more fiddly, fit exhaust pipes made from ⅛ inch brass rod or tube. After cleaning up and painting,

Left: **This CIÉ Bulleid designed 'tin' van was built from Plasticard on a chassis from a Parkside kit for an LMS CCT van.** Peter Swift

add door handles and handrails and interior grilles made from wire and partitions from more Plasticard. For the underframe, remove all boxes, fans and other details. Fit new battery boxes (such as from the ABS range) and remodel the fuel tank from Plasticard. The circular panels can be made using a leather punch. The Mark III based 7601 series EGVs can be produced by a similar method. The Lima Mk III Sleeping car is probably the best donor carriage in this instance.

The tables on pages 21-23 summarise how to produce sets of modern CIÉ/IÉ and NIR locomotive hauled stock.

Numbers	Source	Adaptations/Notes:
3157-3166 Dundalk ('Dutch') heating vans	Lima LMS short brake	The raised body details have to be filed off and new Plasticard overlays produced after making new window apertures in the donor body. Add roof vents and fuel tanks.
3171-92 GSVs	Lima Mk 1 BG	Although the carriages look like full Brakes, they are converted from second hand BR BCK / BSK Mk I carriages which were 63ft 5in long and not 57ft as in a standard BR full Brake. Probably the best option here is to start with the incorrectly long (for BR) Lima BG. Fill in and open up various windows, add roof vents, fuel tanks and B4 pattern bogies.
4101-4114 Standard	Lima/Hornby Mk IIA/B/C	Repaint.
4401-4402 Buffet standard	Lima Mk IIB	Repaint.
4601-4603	Lima LMS short brake	EGVs (conversion from 3157 series 3162/3/6 to run with Mk II stock) Fill in/open up various windows, add roof and side vents, fuel tanks, extend body slightly
5101-6 First	Lima Model MIR Dapol Mk IID FO Lima Mk 2F FO	Commercially available, repaint. Repaint. Commercially available, repaint.
5151-9 Composite	Lima Mk 2F TSO	Alter windows and add centre door.
5201-36 Standard	Lima Model MIR Dapol Mk IID TSO Lima Mk 2F TSO	Commercially available, repaint. Commercially available, repaint. Repaint. Repaint.
5401-11 Restaurant	Lima Mk 2F TSO	Window modifications.
5610-10	Lima Mk 2F FO	EGVs, modify windows, add grilles.
6101-05 Driving brake	Lima Mk 3 TSO	Driving end; modified side windows; extra doors.
6301-19 Standards	Lima Mk 3 TSO	Alternate sliding windows needed.
7101-60 Standards/First/Citygold/ Composites	Lima Mk 3 TSO Lima MIR	Commercially available. Commercially available, repaint.
7161-7162	Lima Mk 3 TSO	Commercially available; for the Executive Coach repaint in the special maroon and black livery.
7163-7164 Standard	Lima Mk 3 TSO	Repaint
7165-7170 Composite	Lima Mk 3 TSO	Repaint
7401-15 Restaurant	Lima Mk 3 RUB	Commercially available; add one extra large window and reduce in size one of the smaller windows.
7601-15 EGVs	Lima Mk 3 SLE	This is the closest match but it needs a lot of work to the windows, grilles and doors.
NIR Stock		Similarly, NIR stock can be built from MIR kits and modified Lima Mk IIB/F vehicles.
546 Grill/Bar/Dining	Lima Mk IIF TSO	Fill in some windows, roof and underframe detail. This was ex-BR RSS M1800, in use from 1982 to 1998 and subsequently sold to Wessex Trains.
547 Grill/Bar/Dining	Lima Mk IIF TSO	Fill in some windows, detail the roof and underframe. This was ex-BR detail Mk IIB supplied new in 1970, withdrawn 1998, now with the RPSI).

Numbers	Source	Adaptations/Notes:
548 (Ex 821) Buffet standard	Lima Mk IIB TSO	Renumbered by 1997, withdrawn in 1996 and now owned by Rail Riders Tours, England.
801 (later 901) Open first (Mk IIB supplied new in 1970)	MIR Lima Mk IIB FO	Commercially available, repaint required.
811	Lima Mk IIB BFK	Driver's windows, corridor connection cover and headlamps need to be added. Converted from a Mk IIB supplied new in 1970.
812 (later 916) Driving brake open standard	Lima Mk IIB BFK	Driver's windows, corridor connection cover and headlamps required. Converted from a Mk IIB supplied new in 1970.
813 (later 917) Driving brake open first	Lima Mk IIB BFK	Add driver's windows, corridor connection cover and headlamps. Converted from a Mk IIC supplied new in 1972.
821 (later 548)	MIR Lima Mk IIB TSO	Commercially available, repaint. Open standard Mk IIB supplied new in 1970, converted to buffet open standard by 1987.
822 (Later 934)	MIR Lima Mk IIB TSO	Commercially available, repaint. Open standard Mk IIB supplied new in 1970.
823 (Later 935) Open standard	MIR Lima Mk IIB TSO	Commercially available, repaint, Mk IIB supplied new in 1970.
824 Open standard	MIR Lima Mk IIB	Commercially available repaint. TSO from a Mk IIB supplied new in 1970. Converted to '80' class trailer standard No 776 in 1984.
825 (Later 932) Open standard	MIR Lima Mk IIB TSO	Commercially available, repaint.
826 Open standard	MIR Lima Mk IIB TSO	Commercially available, repaint, catalogue number C4, (Mk IIC SO supplied new in 1972. Converted to '80' class trailer standard No 778 in 1984).
827	MIR	Commercially available repaint, catalogue number C4, (Mk IIc SO supplied new in 1972. Converted to '80' class trailer standard No 779 in 1984.
828 Open standard	MIR Lima Mk IIB TSO	Commercially available, repaint.. Mk IIC SO supplied new in 1972, converted to '80' class trailer standard No.780 in 1984.
901 (ex 801) First open	MIR Lima Mk IIB FO	Commercially available, repaint. Renumbered in 1981, stored in 1999 and now owned by Rail Riders Tours, England.
902 (later 920) First corridor	MIR Lima Mk IIB FK	Commercially available, repaint. Mk IIB FK, ex BR W13509, introduced 1981.
903 First open	Lima Mk II FO	Mk IIC FO, ex-BR M3166, introduced 1983, stored in 1999 and now owned by Rail Riders Tours, England.
904 First open	Lima Mk IIF FO	Repaint. Mk IIF FO, ex-BR M3367, introduced 1988, withdrawn 1997 and now owned by Rail Riders Tours, England.
911 Brake standard generator van	Lima Mk IIB BFK	Commercially available as a set of 3, although 911 has been modelled incorrectly. Some windows to be filled in, doors removed, grilles and roof mounted silencers added. Mk IIB BFK, ex-BR W14104, introduced 1981. (Formerly a corridor coach, it was converted to an open in 1988). Renumbered 8911 in 2002.
912 Brake first generator van	Lima Mk IIB BFK	Some windows to be filled in, doors removed, grilles and roof mounted and silencers added. Mk IIB BFK, ex-BR W14108, introduced 1981. (Formerly a Standard corridor coach, converted to a First open in 1989).
913 Brake executive generating van	Lima Mk IIB BFK	Some windows filled in, doors removed, grilles and roof mounted silencers added. Mk IIB BFK, ex-BR W14111, introduced 1981. (Formerly a standard corridor coach, converted to an executive coach with loose chairs in 1989. Reverted to BFGV by 1997.)

Numbers	Source	Adaptations/Notes:
914 Brake standard generator van	Lima Mk IIB BFK	Some windows filled in, doors removed, grilles and roof mounted silencers added. (Mk IIB BFK, ex-BR W14110, introduced 1983). (Formerly a corridor coach, it was converted to an open in 1988, withdrawn 1998 and now owned by Rail Riders Tours, England.)
915 Brake first generator van	Lima Mk IIB BFK	Some windows filled in, doors removed, grilles and roof mounted silencers added. Formerly BSGV, converted to BFGV in 1993. Mk IIB BFK, ex BR W14106, introduced 1983. (Formerly a corridor coach, it was converted to an Open in 1989 and to a First open in 1993. Withdrawn 1999, now owned by Rail Riders Tours, England.)
916 (ex 812) Driving brake standard	Lima Mk IIB BFK	Driver's windows, corridor connection cover and headlamp required. Renumbered by 1994, withdrawn 1996, now with the RPSI.
917 (ex 813) Driving brake first	Lima Mk IIB BFK	Driver's windows, corridor connection cover and headlamps. required. Renumbered by 1994, out of service by 1997.
920 (ex 902) Standard	Lima Mk IIB FK	Converted from First to Standard and renumbered in 1991. Withdrawn in 2001 and sold to Wessex Trains.
921-8 Corridor/open standard	Lima MIR	Commercially available as a set of 3. Commercially available, repaint. Mk IIB FKs, ex-BR W13490, Lima Mk IIB FK W13495, W13496, W13508, W13503 W13498, W13506 and W13510, introduced 1981. All but 922 and 928 were converted to Open standards in 1988-89. Nos 922/8 withdrawn in 1994, 921/5 in 1997 and 927 in 1999. Nos 923/4/6 were withdrawn in 2001. Nos 924/6 were sold to Wessex Trains.
929 (later 933) Open standard	Lima Mk IIB TSO	Mk IIC TSO, ex-BR M5577, introduced in 1981.
930-931 Open standard	Lima Mk IIB TSO	Mk IIC TSOs, ex-BR M5573, M5531, introduced in 1981 and withdrawn in 1998.
932 (ex 825) Open standard	MIR Lima Mk IIB TSO	Commercially available, repaint. Mk IIC SO, supplied new 1972. Renumbered in 1986 and withdrawn 1998.
933 (ex 929) Standard	Lima Mk IIB TSO	Mk IIC TSO. (Renumbered by 1987, withdrawn 1998.)
934 – 935 (ex 822 – 823) Standard	MIR Lima Mk IIB TSO	Commercially available, repaint. Withdrawn in 1997, now with the RPSI.
8911	Lima Mk IIB BFK	Formerly No 911, renumbered in 2002. Windows now plated over, it looks similar to the IÉ 5601 series EGVs.
8941-48	Lima Mk.IIF TSO	Former Gatwick Express coaches purchased in 2001. Numbers 72634 (6089), 72637 (6098), 72605 (6082), 72609 (6080), 72626 (6017), 72627 (5974), 72646 (6078) and 72647 (6081).

NIR Railcars

In recent years, of course, NIR services have been dominated by diesel multiple units, and with a little ingenuity they too can be modelled.

80 class DEMUs, (full three-car set)	MIR	MIR etched brass overlays with white metal cab ends and power bogie. Requires donor Lima carriages.
80 class DMBS	Lima class 33 motor bogie Mk IIB or M IIC coaches.	A Brake corridor first is needed for the power car. This requires quite extensive cutting and splicing with Plasticard to get the windows right, and two Open seconds for the driving and intermediate trailers to make a three car train.
752-3	Lima Mk 2B BFK	Fit driving end.
760	Ex NIR 822 (see above)	
774	Lima Mk 2B TSO	
775-80	Ex NIR 823-8 (see above)	

Above: **NIR Hunslet 'DL' class No 101 *Eagle* arriving at Dunmore & Fidlin with a rake of NIR carriages in grey/blue livery. The model is an old resin bodied MIR kit running on a modified Athearn 'F7' chassis. A new highly detailed kit is now available from MIR to fit the Lima BR Class 20 chassis.**

Below: **CIÉ Metropolitan Vickers 'A' class diesel A56 waits in a siding for its next turn of duty on Dunmore & Fidlin. The model is made from a Q Kits white metal kit running on a modified Airfix BR Class 31 chassis.** Both, Stephen Johnson

Opposite page bottom: **Lima Mk IIs can be easily converted to NIR stock. This carriage has been modified at the Brake end to include the generator set with the addition of some suitable etched side grills, whilst the roof has had a well introduced to accommodate the silencers.**
Stephen Johnson

Right: **NIR General Motors-built diesel locomotive No 111 *Great Northern* runs around a train at Dunmore & Fidlin. The locomotive is made from a MIR white metal kit running on a slightly modified Athearn 'SD9' chassis. MIR now offer this kit as a one piece resin moulding. The correct shade of NIR 'Intercity' blue paint, transfers and etched nameplates are all available in the MIR range.**

Below: **A three car NIR '80' class railcar set in its original maroon and blue livery arrives at Dunmore & Fidlin. This MIR kit uses etched brass overlays that are applied to Lima Mk II carriages. The Lima carriages need a little modification to line up the new windows and new cast white metal ends also have to be applied to the carriages.**
Both, Stephen Johnson

Left: **This model of a CIÉ four wheel bulk cement wagon or 'bubble' as they are sometimes referred to, is made from an MIR kit. The two piece resin tank body is assembled and then mounted on a white metal chassis. In real life the 'bubbles' are not usually this clean looking, the cement discolouring them to a grey or grey/white colour, with only the occasional trace of their original colour scheme appearing from under the grime. There is plenty of opportunity for modellers to apply their weathering skills if they are building one of these vehicles.**

Below: **This CIÉ 20 ton goods brake started off life as a Parkside Dundas LNER Brake van kit. With some careful surgery, mainly involving the repositioning of the verandah, a fairly convincing model can be made.** Both, Stephen Johnson

Wagons

Wagons usually attract less attention than coaches, but paradoxically are likely to cause Irish modellers more trouble. Although Irish lines used the same basic designs, box vans, three, five, six and seven plank opens, cattle wagons and goods brakes, as British companies, here the design differences are more pronounced with Irish concerns using simple and rather archaic brake gear, outside W-irons, triangulated underframes and other idiosyncrasies. Most of the broad gauge lines, and some of the narrow, also evolved a very useful, and characteristic, design not found in the rest of Britain: the 'convertible' wagon. This was basically a small covered van, with louvered vents, and the roof in two portions, with an open central section, which could be covered with a tarpaulin. The great idea was that, with the tarpaulin rolled up for better ventilation, the vehicles could also be used for livestock, being thoroughly cleaned with limewash, or later chemical disinfectants, before being used again for general merchandise. Such 'multi-use' vehicles were very useful on Irish lines where there were huge livestock fairs, but the traffic tended to be one way (eastward either to the fattening grounds of Kildare and Meath, or the cross-channel cattle boats) and periodic. Such vehicles however have to be scratch-built. Cast kits are available for a GSR open wagon from Studio Scale Models, which is supplied with alternative buffer castings to build a GNR(I) version of this wagon. They also make an etched brass kit for a GNR(I) goods brake. Jeremy Suter produces a GNR(I) covered van and a UTA (ex-GNR(I)) parcels van. Kits have also been added to this range for GNR(I) and NCC/UTA container wagons and the bread containers which these wagons often carried. Further cast wagon kits are under development. The GNR(I) cattle wagon once made by the Model Wagon Company is now long out of production. A number of cardboard kits for SLNCR wagons and coaches, MGWR six-wheelers and a rather colourful GSWR butter van are included in the Alphagraphix range, but to make them operational, you will need suitable running gear.

Some possible wagon conversions are:

- The Slater's Midland three-plank open is quite close to SLNCR open wagons.
- The Slater's Midland four-plank open and sliding door box van kits are quite close to NCC wagons, but will need outside W-irons. These can be made by cutting down the W-irons sold for compensation wagon chassis, and gluing them outside the moulded plastic axle boxes.
- The Parkside Dundas BR 12-ton plywood body van (ref PC08) is quite like the GNR wagons used for cement traffic, but needs new corrugated ends, mounting on the Ratio 10ft wheelbase chassis, and strictly an altered roof radius.
- The Parkside Dundas LNER van (ref PC06) can be converted into one of the CIÉ 17222 series vans by removing the diagonal bracing, fitting new doors and altering the roof radius.
- The Parkside Dundas LNER 20-ton brake van can be converted to a CIÉ goods brake.
- The Hornby Dublo/Wrenn BR steel van with corrugated ends is quite close to some GNR(I) wagons from the 1950s. The main modification needed is removing the ventilators from the commercial model.
- Charles Roberts Esso tank wagons can be made by widening the Airfix kit and slightly shortening the chassis to move the buffer beams closer to the tank end. By shortening the chassis in the middle, splicing the two sections, re-modelling the brake gear, and fitting a different catwalk, the CIÉ Burmah Oil Company vehicle can also be modelled.
- Lima Seacows and Sealions are not too far from NIR ballast hoppers.

One interesting conversion which can be tackled, is to modify the Hornby (Tri-ang) crane to represent the NCC six-ton hand crane, or the similar GNR(I) version. Dismantle the model and discard the wheels. The chassis needs to be widened by 2mm. Begin with sawing it through length-wise. The inclined portions to hold the crane jib in transit have solid outer faces on the Hornby model, but are open on the prototype, so the excess metal can be filed away. Drill and tap holes for 8BA through each of one pair of axle boxes (if the vehicle is not to be compensated, drill all four axleboxes). Then two rods are glued in to hold the sides at the correct distance, with epoxy resin to provide strength and fill in the gap. The buffers should now be at the correct distance apart of 25mm (6ft 3in). A build up of epoxy in the centre of each end can then be filed to represent the central vertical strut on the GNR crane: this feature is not present in the NCC one. The floor can also by drilled and tapped, to take the vertical brass screw which holds the crane on. Depending on gauge, you will probably need new wheels and bearings. The crane itself needs some modifications. In particular the balance weight should be curved, and bear some detail, such as the cast names of Cowans and Sheldon, and building up the balance weight The crane hawsers should be of wire rather than chain as supplied on the model. It should of course run with either a low-sided or a flat match wagon.

One colourful feature of British operation which the modeller will miss is the private owner wagon which was very rare in Ireland. Recently Bachmann produced a limited run of seven-plank open wagons, authentically finished in the livery used by Murphy Brothers, coal merchants of Waterford. The models were sold in boxed sets of three, with different running numbers.

The modern image modeller is better catered for. A large range of wagons are available from the Model Irish Railways catalogue. These include four wheel and bogie container wagons with a variety of 10ft, 20ft and 40ft ISO containers. Transfers are available to make these up into Bell, B+I and CIÉ containers. Other loads for the four wheel flat wagon include Guinness and acrylonitrile tankers and beer keg containers. The modeller could also look to various containers produced by Bachmann and Hornby to vary the load. Both the four wheel and bogie cement tankers are catered for as well as the bogie fertiliser wagons. Other wagons would present more work in either scratchbuilding or converting existing products or kits.

N Gauge Conversions

There are fewer opportunities for creating Irish models from N gauge equipment, but the Graham Farish '2P' could form the basis of some of the medium sized Irish 4-4-0s, and the same company's four-wheel suburban coaches, with a little splicing and the addition of a centre pair of wheels, make passable models of ex-GSWR six wheel coaches. The full Third is a good match, and can also be converted into a Lavatory composite by sanding off the mouldings for the centre compartment door and blocking up the quarter-lights in that compartment. A Brake third can be made by some more involved cutting and splicing of two Farish brake ends. The chassis will also need lengthening and the insertion of an extra central set of axleguards. The easiest solution to the six-wheel problem is to glue a set of wheels into the central axleguards and file off the flanges, so the wheels are actually clear of the running rails.

Below: **The Bachmann OO gauge model of the Murphy Brothers coal wagon, mentioned in the text, which was commissioned by Murphy Models of Dublin.** Alan O'Rourke

BELL
BELL
BELL
BELL

20
TON
BRAKE
VAN
C
N
41

Opposite page, top: **The colourful petunia and geranium liveried Bell containers were once a common sight on the Irish railway system. These two 20ft containers and their bogie flat wagons are made from MIR kits.** Stephen Johnson

Opposite page, bottom: **This GNR(I) 20 ton Brake is made from a Studio Scale Models etched brass kit. The kit can be made in any of the 4mm gauges and also has etched rocking W-irons for compensation. Some of these Brakes found their way onto the CIÉ system after the dissolution of the GNRB in 1958.** David Malone

This page, top: **GNR(I) four wheel van used in passengers trains modelled as running in UTA days with modified doors. This model in 4mm scale is made from a Jeremy Suter cast kit and includes a compensated chassis and a pre-formed brass roof.** Alan O'Rourke

Centre: **A GNR fitted goods van (right) from a Jeremy Suter kit, and a GSR 'Irish standard open' (left) from an SSM kit. Both these are cast white metal kits and include brass etches to build three-point compensated chassis. The GNR built open wagons to almost exactly the same pattern, the only difference being the buffers. The kits come with two sets of castings for these, allowing you to build either GSR or GNR versions. These kits are to 4mm scale, and can be finished to run on OO, EM, or 21mm gauge track.** Alan O'Rourke

Below: **SLNCR brake van No 2, in 7mm scale, built from an Alphagrafphx card body kit with cast underframe components and Slaters wheels.** Roger Crombleholme

Above: **The Lima models of the BR Sealion and Seacow wagons just need to be repainted to convert them into NIR ballast wagons.** Stephen Johnson

Below: **The Airfix 12 ton box van repainted into CIÉ livery makes a passably effective, although not accurate, model of one of the CIÉ 17222 series wagons.** Stephen Johnson

Above: **Between 1923 and 1925, the MGWR and the GSR bought a total of 27 sets of parts to build some 2-6-0 tender engines. These were made at Woolwich Arsenal in London to an SECR design. In the event, only 26 locomotives were actually built. They became the '372' and '393' classes, the two types having different sizes of driving wheels, though they were all universally known as the Woolwich Moguls. Not long after Bachmann produced a model of the original 'N' class Mogul upon which the Irish machines were based, an Irish version appeared. It was available in CIÉ green, black or weathered black and with a range of numbers.** Stephen Johnson

Below: **A 7mm model of GNR(I) 'U' class No 197 *Lough Neagh*, stands outside Knockmore Junction signal cabin.** Tony Wright, courtesy British Railway Modelling

CHAPTER 4

LAYOUTS

There are a few enthusiasts who are happy to collect or build models, display them in a glass case, and take them for the occasional run at the club or a friend's layout. However, sooner or later most modellers hanker after running their own line, while for others it is the layout that comes first, with locomotives and rolling stock selected to suit. Either way, you soon have to square three circles: what sort of layout you want; how much space you have; and what scale-gauge combination (see Chapter 2) you will use. Space is often the limiting factor. The average modeller probably has a box room, garden shed or part of a garage. Some may have to do with the space on top of a row of book cases, though such sites can make attractive scenic narrow gauge layouts. The lucky few may have an area of maybe 20ft x 20ft or an attic conversion at their disposal. To some extent space determines scale, although some people make very imaginative use of small areas: Richard Chown's Castle Rackrent system, although in what modern modellers regard as the 'large' scale of 7mm:1ft, began as a 16ft x 3ft terminus. You will have to make some fairly binding decisions at an early stage in layout planning. If you want to run eight coach expresses in 4mm scale, you cannot do it with 3ft passing loops! There are plenty of good books on the market dealing with the generic skills of building base boards, laying track, wiring up layouts and operating points and signals by mechanical or electrical methods, so we will not repeat these methods here. Rather, in the next two chapters we will move off the footplate and look at providing somewhere suitable to run your Irish models.

Left: **Loughrea station in August 1975, with No G613 bringing its single coach train in from Attymon Junction. Other than the rolling stock, and partial re-laying with second hand bullhead rail, the scene is much as it was when the line opened in 1890.** Paul Taylor

The first phase is choosing and planning your layout. Basically you have several options. The first of these is to design your own track plan from scratch. This has the advantage of allowing you to adapt it to space and personal taste, but disregarding the usual rules may make for a very odd, unrealistic-looking track plan. You can of course often find justification in the prototype. For instance, a basic rule for a terminus is to have a run-round loop to allow the engine from an arriving train to get to the other end. Leaving this out will cause all sorts of problems, though the North British Railway did it at Eyemouth in Berwickshire, where the station was on a gradient, and running round was achieved by gravity shunting under the control of the guard's handbrake!

The second option is to adapt a prototype, probably the most common solution. Select a favourite location and adapt it to suit your space, usually by tightening some of the curves, shortening platforms and loops and simplifying some of the sidings (much of this has actually happened at many Irish stations over the past 30 years under the label of rationalisation!). You can always invent a suitable location for your modified station: possibly some fictitious border location with combined GSR/GNR(I) or CIÉ/UTA running powers, allowing for an interesting mix of stock. Those who know a bit more about Irish railway history may prefer to model one of the many 'might have been' railway schemes that never got past the planning phase such as the Waterford & Central Ireland Railway's plan to extend from Mountmellick to Mullingar, the various schemes to

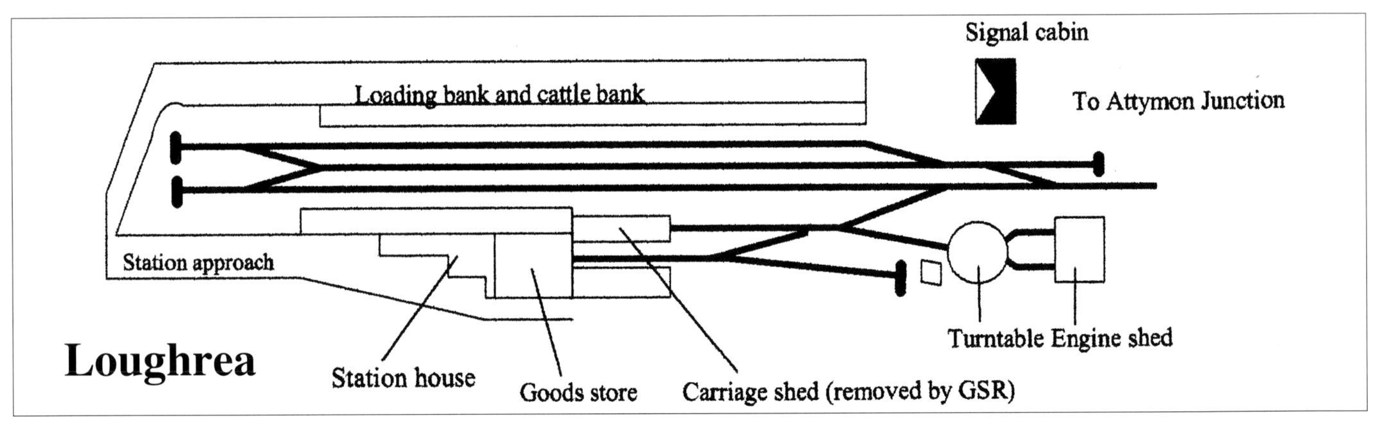

develop Belmullet as a transatlantic port, with rail connections to either Westport or Ballina, or the narrow gauge Ulster & Connaught scheme, which would have stretched from Newry to Galway.

A third option is to build an exact replica of a specific location. This is relatively rarely pursued in its pure form, where the modeller sets out to recreate a three-dimensional railway scene, from a specific time, using only locomotive classes and rolling stock which ran on the line at that period, with a suitable timetable sequence, and all buildings, signals and other fixtures congruent for a specific period. Sitting by such a piece of work is about as close as you can get to railway scenes of say 90 years ago. But, you need a good deal of research, and even relatively simple models can need a lot of space if built exactly to scale. In England, even quite minor stations often had extensive siding and yard space, but in comparison, Irish country locations had very simple track plans, such that the modeller may be tempted to add a few points! However, the ground space occupied by even quite simple layouts was often considerable.

In practice, it is often unnecessary to be too tied to a historical period, for the simple reason that many locations, especially in rural Ireland, changed very little from their opening until closure or modernisation in the 1960s or 1970s. Indeed, away from the main lines, most stations reached a fairly traditional style of signalling and architecture, which changed little if at all from the 1890s to the 1960s. With duplicate sets of rolling stock, you could run the same model as set in 1900, 1920, 1940 or 1960. In the rest of the chapter, we will present several locations as typical of Irish practice, to provide a range of potential prototypes.

The branch terminus: Loughrea

In an attempt to escape the accusation of 'playing with a train set', the first thing many modellers do to get away from the basic oval is to build a simple end-to-end scheme, following the idea that 'real' trains run from A to B, rather than in circles. About half of such a design is usually scenically developed and on view to the public; the other half is taken up by a fan of hidden sidings ('the fiddle yard') representing the rest of the railway network. Logically, we have now moved from a train that chases its tail to one that runs up and down a glorified siding with a bit of shunting at the ends! The branch line terminus has however been the mainstay of railway modelling for about 50 years, based it seems on the assumptions that such layouts are easy to build, require little rolling stock (pertinent for Irish examples where most equipment has to be scratch-built or heavily modified) and quick to get operational. All are true, to some extent. Richard Chown claimed he could provide an interesting sequence at Castle Rackrent with two engines, two coaches and eight wagons. However, activity at the typical Irish branch terminus was rather limited with, on most days, between two and five passenger trains arriving, running round and departing. One or two of these might be mixed, conveying goods traffic as well, and generating some shunting. Of course, you can build such a layout and amuse yourself by running an intensive suburban service, with large tender engines, but it will look odd!

Above: **Loughrea station house and goods store, from the approach road, seen in August 1975.** Paul Taylor

A little local knowledge (the sort that can be gleaned from working timetables and weekly notices) can allow more variation. If your period included the era when Irish railways handled much livestock, the monthly fair will be an excuse to run in two or three specials of empty cattle wagons the day before, loaded and dispatched after the fair. In the sugar beet season, you can have the branch engine work an overload goods up the junction in the evening, or maybe a dedicated beet special starting from your station. Public holidays, seaside excursions and GAA matches will all provide excuses for extra passenger workings. A few branches also had an independent goods train running through from a nearby large station, such as Newmarket which had a daily goods to and from Mallow. One other branches, such as the GNR line to Belturbet, you may be able to include a rail connected source of mineral or industrial traffic.

Loughrea is the quintessential Irish branch terminus, compactly providing the usual facilities of passenger accommodation, a small goods yard, engine shed, run-round loop and a loading bank for livestock. However, be warned that such rural stations, however simple the track plan, were often very spread out, as land was cheap. The station and yard at Loughrea occupied an area 1,300ft long, with maximum width of about 150ft, which in 4mm requires a space measuring some 17ft x 2ft. However, if you are willing to compromise on train size, such layouts can usually be compressed, especially in length, without losing too much character. In fact, urban termini were often much more cramped, and resorted to the sort of space saving dodges modellers have used for many years, like three-way points or traversers.

Another option for small layouts, especially if you like more than one company, is to make duplicate models of the main railway buildings such as the station house, goods store and signal box, each set in the style of a particular company, secured to the baseboards by plug fittings, rather than glued in place. Thus, in a few minutes, the ashlar stone of a Midland station can be changed for the engineers' yellow brick of the GNR(I). The only unusual feature about Loughrea was the useful Y-formation on the loop, allowing engines to be released either from the platform or loading bank though this was removed in the last years as cattle traffic declined.

Such small layouts can be quickly built. Wiring is usually very simple as long as you use self-isolating points: a couple of feeds and maybe one or two sections that can be switched off to isolate engines. Signalling is also usually unsophisticated. The Board of Trade could usually be satisfied by a small ground frame for a home and a starting signal and those points that ran directly off the running road, with the others operated by local levers. The only problem is disguising the 'hole in the sky' where the train dives out of view: a good scenic break can usually be made from an overbridge, which was a very common feature of Irish prototypes; tunnels, much beloved in OO gauge, are very rare in Irish practice.

There are of course variants on this theme. One would be Foynes, where the branch terminated at the quayside, and the baseboard can be finished as a wharf, or those with a penchant for maritime modelling could indulge in building one or two small coastal vessels. Foynes also had sidings for oil and fertiliser traffic, so providing opportunities for those who like goods train operation.

A small halt: Spa (Fenit branch)

This shows just how small Irish stations can be. Some were even smaller: just a platform and a cottage, and of course, on some lines, in later years, railcars might call at certain level crossings by request. Such a small prototype is most useful either as a static diorama, or as a second station on a larger layout. The trackwork allows trains in either direction to shunt: one going to Fenit can stop at the platform and shunt wagons to or from siding Y; one going in the opposite direction can pull up before the points and shunt to and from X. However, getting a wagon from X onto a train going to Fenit is problematic! In real life, there were dodges, such as borrowing a horse or using a tow rope between the wagon and an engine on a parallel line. Such small stations were rarely block posts, although they might have signals to protect a level crossing or where trains called by request only, to indicate that there were passengers waiting. The track plan meant that the company only had the expense of providing one turnout with proper safety devices. In practice, the points were usually worked from a ground frame, but the crew had to insert the staff for the section to release this and enable shunting to occur.

A small passing station: Rathkeale

The next stage on from the branch terminus is often a through station. You can add another fiddle yard, but this means that up to two-thirds of your layout will be hidden, so at this stage most modellers make both ends meet, and go back to the oval. The hidden yard is now a series of loops, such that trains can arrive or depart from either end. The typical small station has a signal box and is a block post. Usually, this means it has a passing loop, so that an up and down train can pass without shunting, or a passenger train can overtake a goods train going in the same direction. Not all block posts had loops, however, and at some one train had to set back into a siding. Usually, this was a goods and except under exceptional circumstances, two passenger trains could not be crossed at such locations.

Rathkeale was unusual in that it had a loop, but only one platform. In practice, the usual crossings here were a goods and a passenger, but on rare occasions two passenger trains crossed, with one held in the loop until the platform was clear. The siding at the east side of the overbridge was added in 1907, and lifted sometime in the early 1950s. At one time there may have been a cattle bank on it. Since the signals only applied to the running road, I assume that goods trains were flagged in and out of the loop by the signal man, while the passenger train ran through. On the rarer occasions when two passenger services crossed, one also had to be hand-signalled in and out of the loop. The station had a carriage dock, a 221ft long platform, a store, loading bank, cattle pens and a 5,400-gallon water tank serving two columns. As a model, it would suit a long thin site, with the overbridge making a good scenic break.

This is also an example of a small station which periodically generated huge flows of livestock. For fairs at Rathkeale, up to three early morning specials of empty wagons ran from Limerick. Sometimes an engine and van followed, with up to four loaded specials back from 10am onwards. The big autumn fairs dispatched up to 80, and on one occasion 120 wagons. The goods facilities were slightly modernised in the 1960s when a gantry crane for containers was installed. Other than that, the services were typical of most Irish secondary lines with three or four passenger trains and one goods each way, with specials for seasonal or excursion traffic. The purpose of the end loading dock was that in the steam era, many passenger trains conveyed stock such as horse boxes, milk vans and ventilated meat and fish wagons, which did not have passenger accommodation, but because they were fitted with continuous brakes, they could run at passenger train speeds. These vehicles were shunted at intermediate stations to and from such docks for loading or unloading.

Another option for such wayside stations is to have a mix of local and fast trains, which pass through at some speed. An example would be one of the intermediate stations on the South Wexford line

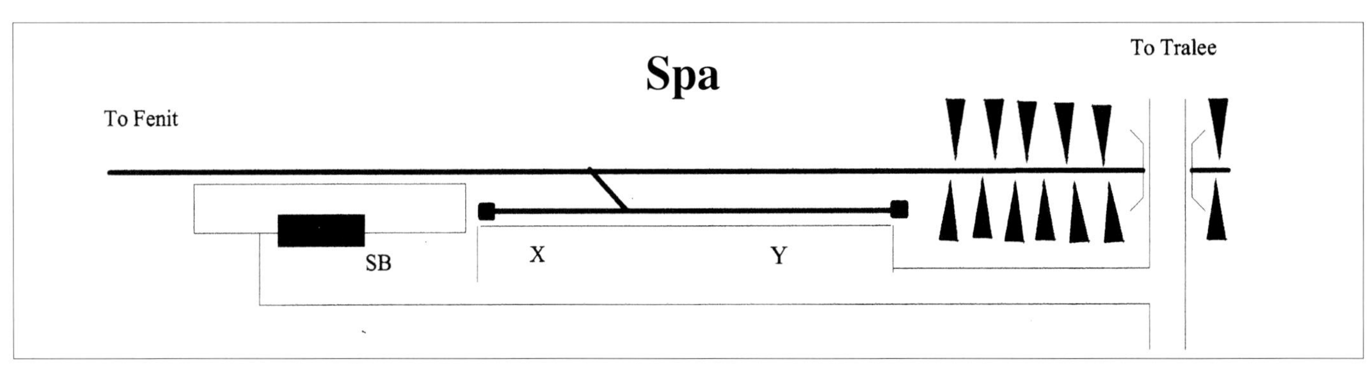

Right: **Rathkeale station, looking towards Limerick, seen in 1979.** Adrian Vaughan collection

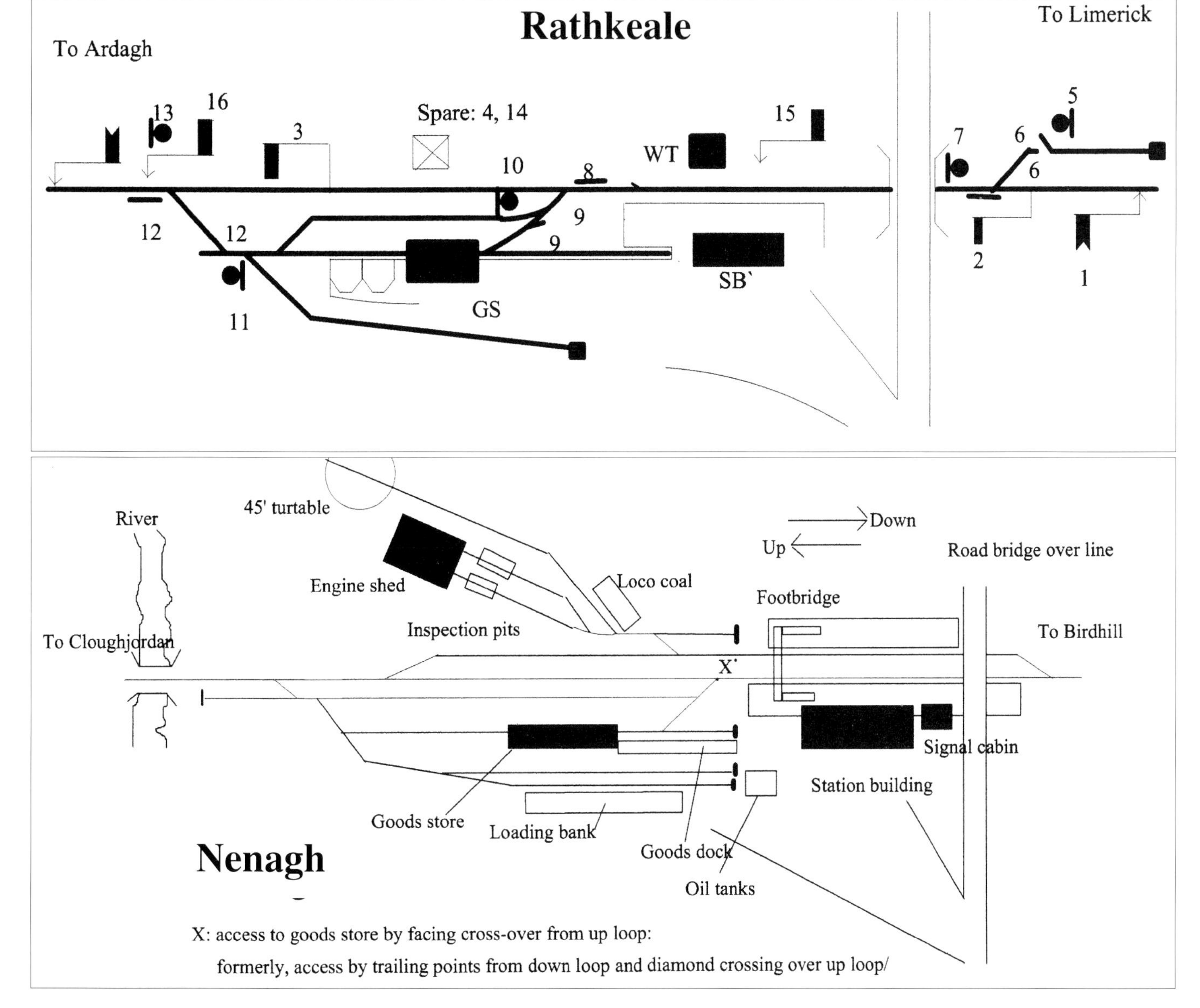

from Rosslare to Waterford, where the three or four stopping trains were augmented by the Rosslare Express to and from Cork, sometimes running in two portions. Where that station serves a medium-sized town, you can also have 'short' workings, from the nearest city which terminate, run round and go back.

A medium-sized through station: Nenagh

Nenagh is a more substantial railhead than Rathkeale. Although not a junction, it had a fully equipped locomotive depot and engines shedded there each night. Here, access to a working timetable will prove useful. For Nenagh, we include summaries of the timetables from the GSR, early and later CIÉ periods, to give some idea of the sort of sequence that could be run on this type of model to provide a prototype service. Again, passenger excursions and livestock fairs will generate extra trains. Among the services listed below are trains from Limerick to Ballybrophy passing through, some continuing on to Dublin, short workings to and from Limerick for local traffic, a light goods to Limerick and the more substantial through Dublin goods, which terminates here with the engine going on shed before working back.

Nenagh; train services 1933.
(departure times are quoted)
7.30am, passenger to Ballybrophy
8.00am, passenger to Limerick
8.40am, goods from Dublin (terminates here)
9.37am, passenger from Ballybrophy (terminates)
10.10am, passenger Limerick-Ballybrophy
11.15am, goods to Limerick
12.17pm, passenger Ballybrophy Limerick
4.56pm, passenger Limerick-Ballybrophy
5.30pm, cattle special to Dublin (Tuesday only)
6.20pm, goods from Limerick (terminates)
7.15pm, passenger from Limerick (terminates here; by 1939, this ran as a mixed train as required)
7.30pm, cattle special from Dublin (Mondays only)
7.48pm, passenger Ballybrophy-Limerick
8.15pm, goods to Dublin

Nenagh; train services 1952.
7.25am, goods from Dublin (terminates)
8.05am, passenger to Limerick
8.56am, passenger Limerick-Ballybrophy
11.35am, goods from Limerick (terminates)
12.39pm, passenger Ballybrophy-Limerick
2.45pm, goods to Limerick
4.04pm, passenger Limerick-Ballybrophy
7.20pm, passenger from Limerick (terminates)
8.19pm, passenger Ballybrophy-Limerick
10.15pm, goods to Dublin

Nenagh; train services 1978.
12.01am, liner to Ballybrophy
9.07am, passenger Limerick-Ballybrophy
12.28pm, passenger Ballybrophy-Limerick
4.15pm, passenger Limerick-Ballybrophy
5.40pm, Limerick-Kingscourt empty gypsum (runs Tuesdays, Thursdays and Saturdays only)
8.43pm, passenger Ballybrophy-Limerick
11.35pm, liner from Ballybrophy

A larger main line station: Ballybrophy

Ballybrophy is a large station, shown here before it was re-signalled. Trains from Nenagh used the bay, with cross platform transfer to the Dublin service, but trains to Nenagh departed from the far side of the island platform, to save passengers off the down train from having to cross the bridge. At one time, the pointwork allowed direct access from the island platform to the branch, but latterly, the branch train had to reverse down the main line in the direction of Cork to clear the points, and then having 'got the disc' headed up the main line 'wrong road' and onto the branch. A layout like this can use a lot of space and a lot of stock, so unless you have a very large room, or build it as a club project, it is not practical except in N gauge. You can have a wide variety of trains. These include: stopping and express main line passenger services (although in steam days practically all trains called here); fast main line goods; locals to and from the Nenagh road; through Dublin to Limerick via Nenagh services (requiring the locomotive to run round and in steam days to be turned); a variety of goods and cattle trains; occasionally the Inchicore trial train for ex-works stock might appear; slow main line trains looped in the offside island platform to be overtaken; engineers specials; ballast trains; beet specials to the Thurles sugar factory; GAA excursions to the big match in Dublin. Incidentally, Ballybrophy itself produced little traffic (from the footbridge you can still see only about a dozen houses!), except for the livestock from Rathdowney fair, for which it was the railhead.

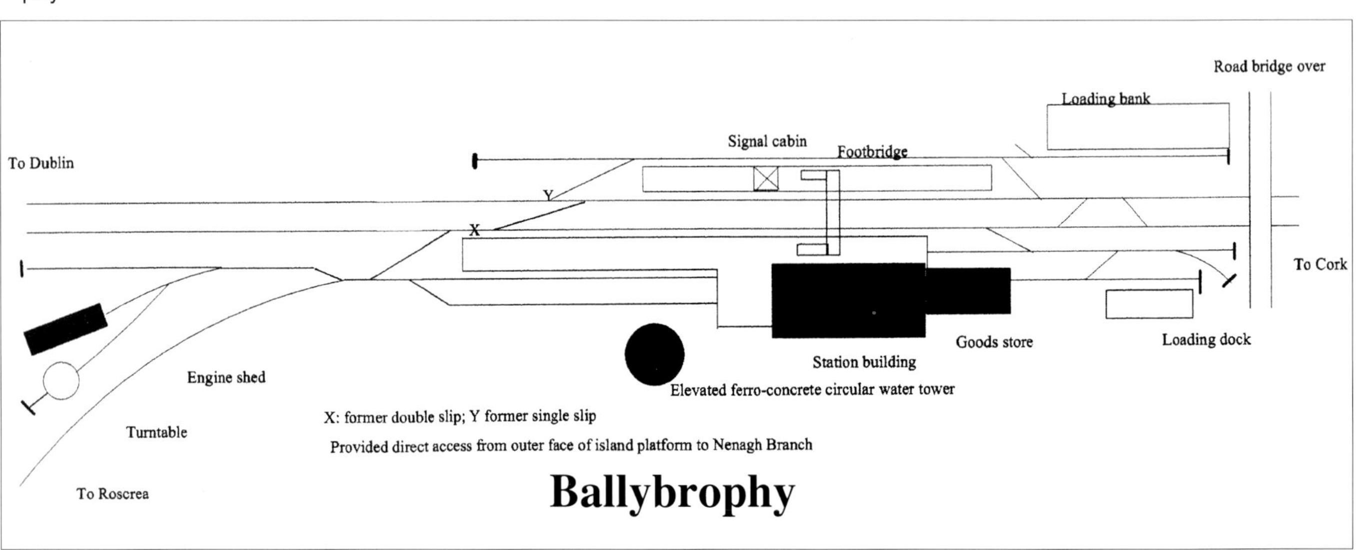

Right: **A view of Rush & Lusk station looking north in 1984. The station, located on the former GNR(I) main line north of Dublin, boasts a typical GNR signal cabin and lower quadrant signals. One feature of this station was the sight of a GNR or later, as here, a CIÉ bus in the station forecourt. One of the long offshoots of the Dublin city bus network terminated here, a working which was inherited by CIÉ from the GNR.** Alan O'Rourke

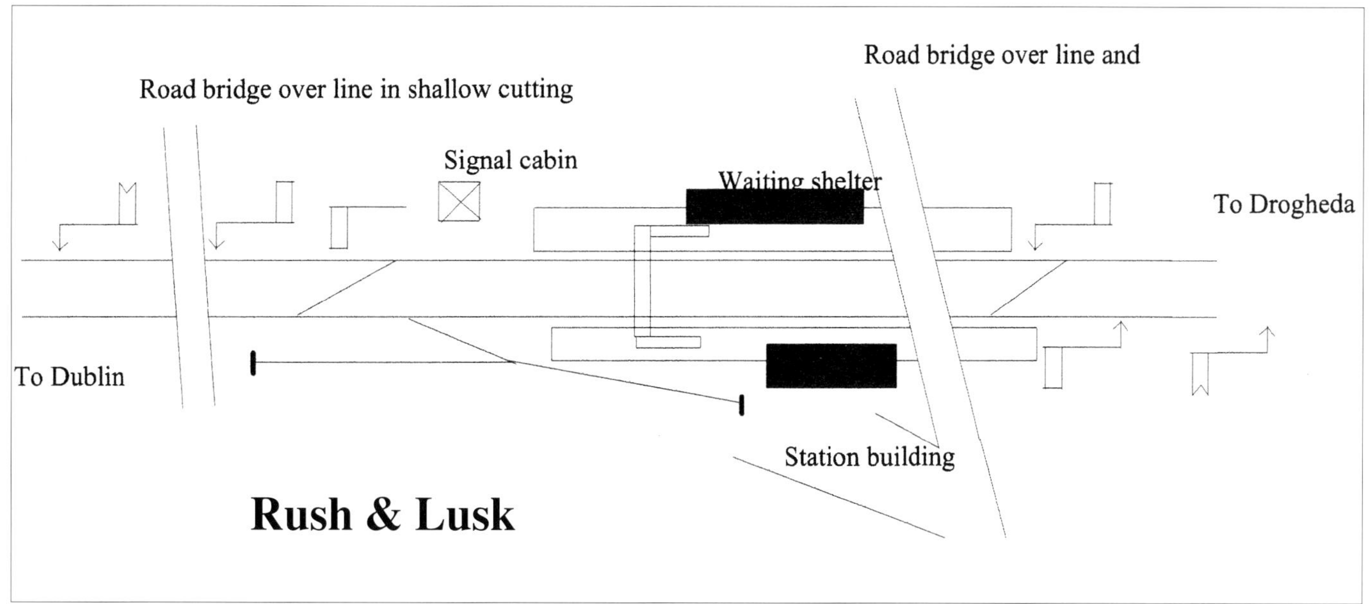

An outer suburban station: Rush & Lusk

If you have room for a double track circuit, but limited space for large station layouts, a good option is to model one of the smaller wayside stations, or an outer suburban stopping place that will justify a fairly frequent service. Here you can have quite a mix of services. Among the workings which could be seen at a location like Rush & Lusk were local stopping passenger, including possibly one or two peak hour services which could terminate here before returning to Dublin. If you are modelling the steam era, you would need at least two cross-overs for running round though for multiple units, a single connection between up and down line will suffice. In addition to local trains, express passenger workings would run straight through.

Some secondary main line passenger might call, maybe including the Night Mails possibly with a long tail of vans for perishable and parcels traffic.

Other traffic would include relief and excursion trains at holiday periods, heavy main line goods and one or two pick up goods each way which stopped to shunt the yard. As always in Ireland cattle specials to the nearest port are likely. Perhaps there would be some mineral trains and fast 'fitted' goods workings consisting of piped or continuously braked vehicles. You can also introduce occasional weekend engineering work, with single line working on one or other side of the station, and if you add a refuge loop or siding, slow goods trains can be held there and overtaken by faster services. For the modern image modeller, a mix of multiple unit local services, locomotive hauled inter-city services and block freights can be run.

This sort of layout can be approached in two ways: as a background for the builder and collector of locomotives to display them against or for the timetable fan to recreate a day's services, and 'watch the trains go by'. For the latter, extensive storage loops would be needed and the frequent re-use of coaching stock, possibly with numerous re-marshalling and maybe alternative numbering on the two sides to disguise this.

A mixed gauge station: Belturbet

One way of capturing the best of both Irish railway worlds is to have both broad and narrow gauge trains running on the same layout in the form of a mixed gauge station. Plenty of examples exist on the prototype such as Strabane, Tynan, Maguiresbridge, Ennis, Dromod and Skibbereen. There are two basic types of mixed gauge station: the through broad gauge route with a narrow gauge terminus, or a location, such as that featured here, where both broad and narrow gauge lines terminate. As always, space is a problem for the modeller, but at a relatively small interchange station such as that at Belturbet at the eastern end of

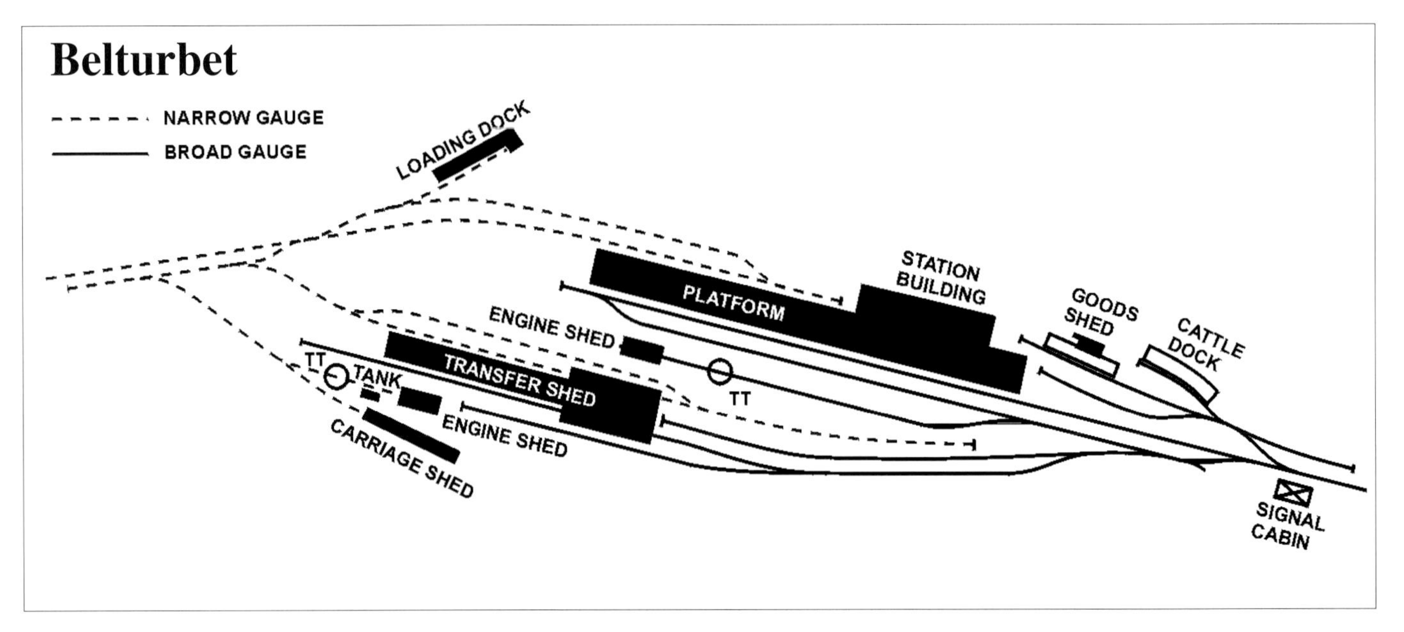

Left: **At Belturbet, the C&L narrow gauge line from Dromod met the GNR branch from Ballyhaise on its Clones to Cavan route. Here GNR 'JT' class 2-4-2T No 94 is seen beside one of the ex-Cork, Blackrock & Passage 2-4-Ts sent north by the GSR when the the Cork line closed in 1932.**
Ian Allan Library

the Cavan & Leitrim Railway, a lot of activity can be packed into a relatively small area.

Here, a Great Northern Railway branch line ran from a junction at Ballyhaise on the Clones to Cavan line, terminating alongside the Cavan & Leitrim narrow gauge line from Dromod. Passenger trains on both gauges ran into opposite ends and opposite sides of the single platform at the GNR station. There was also a goods transfer shed served by both gauges and a small locomotive shed. One effective way of operating such a layout is to have an oval type track plan, but with the narrow gauge running off one way to fiddle sidings at the back of the layout. The broad gauge line can run off in the opposite direction to the back to more fiddle sidings adjacent to the narrow gauge. Now although Belturbet is a specific location with two distinct companies, one does have the freedom, or modeller's licence if you prefer, to run just about any combination. Another advantage of such a location is that the trains would be on the short side, being branch line trains. A further source of interest for the modeller here is the coal traffic which was handled at this location. Narrow gauge trains brought coal from the mines at Arigna to Belturbet. The coal then had to be shovelled by hand into broad gauge wagon, to reach its final destination. In later years, this was often the cement factory at Drogheda. At no time was the handling of coal traffic at either end of the C&L line ever mechanised. The plan above gives some idea of the track layout at Belturbet.

An industrial location

Some modellers delight in adapting unusual prototypes, which were usually kept well away from the public gaze, such as branches and sidings to factories, docks, quarries, mines and such industrial locations. In Britain, such lines usually handled goods trains only, and often had their own locomotives. For much of the railway age, Ireland was primarily an agricultural country, and such systems were rarer. Some stations did have facilities used by private industry. Foynes has already been mentioned as a small terminus with extensive facilities to handle various types of goods traffic. There were depots for coal and fertilisers and later sidings serving oil storage depots. A number of short extensions were laid in different parts of Ireland, to tap mineral deposits, most notably that from Arigna to Aughabehy on the Cavan & Leitrim system, the Castlecomber and Deerpark branch in Kilkenny and the Wolfhill line in Laois, all built to serve collieries. The last mentioned also served an asbestos factory.

Several railway companies also built lines to tap sources of ballast for the permanent way. In some cases, the company just bought land adjacent to the running line, put in a siding and removed the stone until the pit was exhausted. The GSWR,

MGWR and GNR(I) also had large permanent installations where they quarried rock and crushed it. These sites, places like Lisduff on the Cork line, Lecarrow on the Mayo branch and Goraghwood on the GNR main line, had substantial plant and buildings for processing and loading the ballast.

Where such sidings and industrial lines left the main network at stations, entry to them was controlled from the signal cabin, usually with a trap point on the siding to stop runaways, and maybe disc shunting signals to control exit and entry. Since such lines did not carry passenger services, they were not subject to scrutiny by the Board of Trade, and so did not need full signalling and interlocking. They were usually worked on the one engine in steam principle, with the crew operating level crossing gates and points from local levers and there was little if any signalling. In some cases, these sidings diverged from running lines between stations, and where maybe only one daily train worked the siding, the building of a special signal cabin to control it was too extravagant. Here, the usual system was to have a ground frame controlling the points into the siding. This was secured in some way, with the points set for the running line, and held there by a locking device. On single lines, the staff for the section might incorporate the key to unlock the ground frame. The train crew had to release the ground frame to shunt the siding. All levers had to be back to normal before the crew could remove the staff and proceed to the end of the section. This caused problems where the train needed to spend some time shunting, as it blocked the section until the staff got back to one end. On lines equipped with ETS, the ground frame sometimes had a subsidiary instrument attached. This allowed the goods train to gain access to the siding, lock itself in, restore all levers to normal, and then the guard could insert the staff into the subsidiary instrument, putting the magazines at each end of the section back in sequence. This effectively cleared the section, allowing further trains to run through it, with the goods train safely out of the way. When shunting was complete, the process was reversed, with the guard taking the staff out of the subsidiary magazine to allow use of the ground frame. The section, was then blocked until the train had reached one end. Examples of such sidings on the GSR with these subsidiary instruments included those which served the sugar factory on the Carlow to Magenay section and Webb's Mills, between Mallow and Lombardstown.

Another intermediate siding was at Balleece, on the Rathdrum to Avoca section of the DSER, which served a quarry. This was an example of such a facility where there was no run-round loop. Empty wagons could be hauled by the engine from Rathdrum station. The rules allowed such trains to run without a brake van. Because of the gradients on this section, the wagons had to be placed in the siding and have their brakes pinned down before uncoupling the engine. Loaded wagons from the siding could be propelled back to Rathdrum with the engine in the rear. Up to 12 empty or 10 loaded wagons could be handled in this way. If more offered, the engine had to make a second run and reassemble the train in the yard at Rathdrum.

Although freight traffic on the Irish network has declined in recent years, some of the industrial locations which remain active are listed below.

- Castlemungret, Limerick: a large cement factory, with special facilities for unloading oil, shale, and (until rail haulage ceased in 2001), gypsum, and loading bagged and bulk cement. Originally, the factory was served by a spur off the North Kerry line, but more recently it has had its own separate line to the Check Cabin at Limerick, worked as a siding by telephone communication between the signal man at the Check and the shunter at Mungret.
- Platin Cement Factory: near Drogheda.
- Tara Mines: near Navan served by the stub of the former Oldcastle branch.
- Kilmastulla Shale Siding: near Birdhill. Since this diverges from a passenger line, although not a block post, the siding is protected by up and down two-aspect colour light home and distant signals. Access is rather oddly by a Y-point, leading to a siding parallel to the running road, off which further sidings trail back to the loading bank.

Although purely industrial railways are less common in Ireland, one quite large system has caught the attention of railway enthusiasts. This is the extensive 3ft narrow gauge network of Bord na Móna. With some 1,000 miles of track and 350 locomotives around the country, these narrow gauge lines transport peat from the bogs to various locations including power stations, briquette works and horticultural bagging plants. Although building a power station may be a bit daunting, the depots can make interesting models. There are a few locations around the country where these narrow gauge lines pass under the broad gauge main lines, opening up interesting possibilities. One drawback is that the only commercially available kit is a 16mm scale Hunslet *Wagonmaster* locomotive made by Essel Engineering. So, just about everything has to be scratch-built. However, for the modeller requiring a

Left: **Irish railway architecture could be on an impressive scale, such as Sancton Woods' designs for the early GSWR stations. This is the building on the up platform at Portarlington.** Alan O'Rourke

Top left: **Even smaller wayside stations were often minor architectural gems in their own right. These are the main building at Moate on the former MGWR Mullingar to Athlone line, photographed in 1984.**

Below left: **This attractive wooden waiting shelter was on the opposite platform at Moate in 1984. Although the line had only one daily passenger train each way by then, the platforms were still well kept with flower beds. Modellers with horticultural interests take note!**
Both, Alan O'Rourke

challenge and something unusual, Bord na Móna offers something different with its diminutive locomotives in chocolate and cream livery and aluminium wagons (see Chapter 6 for further details).

Drawings for Irish railway buildings are even scarcer than for rolling stock. A handful have been published over the years and a few more can be found in old engineering journals, but as a basic rule, the best way to get started is: if it's still standing get photographs and some dimensions with a tape or a pole marked in feet. There is however quite a range of cardboard kits in both 4mm and 7mm scales, manufactured by Alphagraphix, of Birmingham, covering both railway and domestic structures. The range now includes station houses, signal cabins, goods stores and line-side cottages. Kits from the 7mm range are available in 4mm for an extra £1.00. The main problem is that the card is rather thin. Some scrap is provided for bracing, but if you want a durable structure, back all external walls with the thickest card you have to hand, and fit internal false ceilings and walls. The extra depth will also add realism around doors and window rebates. Don't forget to colour cut edges with felt tip or matt paint, or you get lots of white lines, and when inserting internal braces from card, make sure you cut ventilation holes to avoid creating any closed compartments that may later warp. Some of the kits lend themselves readily to adaptation, such as the station house from Dromod (Cavan & Leitrim Railway) which is really in three sections: a single-storey station office, a two-storey house and a yard/lavatory block, which provides opportunities for splicing and kit-bashing. The only tricky bit is cutting out the window arches. Use a good sharp scalpel blade, take your time and you will get good results. The kits come with printed windows, but if you want to invest some more time, you can glaze with either microscope glass (with the glazing bars scribed on, using engraving tools which can be bought from handicraft shops) or thin perspex (with the glazing bars built up from thin strips of Plasticard), recessing the bottom panes by an extra thickness of card to get a realistic sash window effect. Extra details such as guttering and fall pipes can also be added from plastic rodding or round section wire.

The trade makes various printed sheets for tiles, slates, brick, stone and moulded plastic sheets for brick and roofing which are suitable for Irish structures. The most characteristic feature of many Irish stations is the use of cut stone. A number of building papers and embossed Plasticard sheets are reasonably close, such as Superquick building paper D8 (grey ashlar), Slaters Plasticard 0419, 0420, 0424 and 0425 embossed sheets, or Wills SSMP200 and SSMP202. Away from the railway, scenery often needs random stone effects (such as the dry stone walls surrounding the fields in the west of Ireland), or cut stone gateposts. These can be moulded from fire-cement quite easily, using one of the readily available brands or a modelling clay such as Das. Several layouts have used a traditional Irish street scene, with painted shop signs, as a backdrop, and good descriptions and illustrations of domestic architecture are provided in these two books:

Irish Countryside Buildings, Shaffrey P & Shaffrey M (Dublin)(1985) O'Brien Press

Buildings of Irish Towns Dublin Shaffrey P & Shaffrey M (Dublin) (1983) O'Brien Press

Some commercial kits for houses, factories and other line-side buildings are also adaptable for Irish layouts, such as the Faller HO scale thatched cottages Nos 278 and 279. For GSR and CIÉ stations don't forget the bilingual name-board and notices, the earlier ones in Celtic script. For Gaelic style lettering, use the Letraset sheets for American Unical font, and a variety of Celtic fonts. Family coats of arms and Celtic images can be downloaded from the website:
www.ireland-information.com/freecelticfonts.htm

Top right: **In the days when most goods went by rail, many stations had commodious goods stores, with a siding running through, such that wagons could be loaded and unloaded under cover. This is the goods shed at Enniscorthy, in 1996. Note the crane on the loading bank beside the store.** Alan O'Rourke

Below right: **The MGWR goods store at Dromod, on the Mullingar to Sligo line, was built to the design of the company's architect, George Wilkinson. This model, based on the building at Dromod, was built using Plasticard, in 4mm scale by David Malone, who also took this photograph of his handiwork.**

Bottom: **Styles of architecture often varied along the course of one line. The station at Bagenalstown, on the Irish South Eastern Railway's Carlow to Kilkenny line, was built in the baroque fashion. It is seen here in a photograph taken in 1981.** Alan O'Rourke

CHAPTER 5

SIGNALLING & OPERATION

As with other aspects of railway operation, Irish signalling tended to follow British practice, but with its own idiosyncrasies. Up to the mid-19th century, signals, such as they existed, and points, were operated from local levers, with much control by hand signalling, allowing trains to follow each other at specified time intervals. With the increasing speed and weight of trains, engineers devised more sophisticated mechanical devices to control movements. It was an accident on Irish soil, the disastrous runaway at Armagh in 1889, that led to the statutory enforcement of the principles of modern signalling. One of these was the use of block signalling. A line was divided into block sections, usually from one signal box to the next. Only one train was allowed in each section at a time. Another was the interlocking of signal cabins, so that signals could not be cleared for conflicting movements or if the points were not correctly set. Incidentally, the term 'signal box' is British terminology; in Ireland, 'signal cabin' is more usual.

Most companies had by then adopted lower quadrant signals, the arm falling between 30 and 60 degrees from the horizontal to indicate clear, of two patterns: stop signals (which normally could not be passed in the horizontal danger position) and distant signals, where the horizontal position indicated a need to stop shortly but not immediately, and could be passed at a reduced speed. The only distinction between these on many lines was cutting a V-shaped notch (the 'fish-tail') in the outer end of the arm of the distant signals. Other than that, the driver's route knowledge was expected to cover the location and type of all the signals.

For single lines, various staffs or tokens were used to provide the driver with authority to enter each block section. The problem was that up and down trains had to alternate, or the staff ended up at the wrong end. To cope with this problem, there were various refinements. First came the staff-and-ticket system, where the drivers of the first trains in the same direction were shown the staff and given a ticket (from a locked box released by a key on the staff) authorising them to proceed, the final train taking the staff to the other end for the next train in the opposite direction. Later the electric train staff (ETS) was developed, where there were multiple staffs in paired magazines at each end of the block section, interlocked so that only one could be out of the magazines at any one time. By the 1890s, signalling technology was moving towards the electro-mechanical era, and on some sections of Ireland's railways such systems still provide safe and effective train control.

The GSR tended to replace pre-1925 signals with GSWR pattern lower quadrants on tapering timber posts, while introducing its own pattern ferro-concrete post cast in one piece. Just before World War 2, a modern steel tubular post was introduced. About this time, a steel arm, with a shallow 'V' shape in cross-section, began to replace the older wooden arms. A few older types however survive. On the former DSER line, there are semaphores on iron lattice posts, similar to those seen in parts of Scotland and on the former London & South Western and South Eastern & Chatham lines in England. Here and there you may still find older cast iron posts, with odd lozenge shaped flat sections in the upright. This design suggests it might originally have been devised to accept the obsolete nineteenth century signal where the arm slotted into the post to indicate clear.

Most companies bought their signalling equipment, either ready made or as component parts, from the commercial suppliers, such as the Railway Signal Company, Saxby & Farmer, McKenzie & Holland, Duttons or Stevens of Worcester. Most Irish companies used one or more of these suppliers and some of their standard parts are available in etches or castings from S&D Models, the Tyrconnel range marketed by Alphagraphix, the Model Signal Company, Scale Signal Supply and Model Signal Engineering (MSE). Typical GSWR /GSR/CIÉ home signals can be made up from parts of the MSE range. The early patterns had square wooden posts, but in 1938, a new design on steel tubular posts was introduced. The Saxby & Farmer arms S0010 can be used. On later period signals on tubular steel posts, a horizontal bend must be made along the axis of the arm. The back blinder normally comes on the etch containing the arms. Various brass tube, rod and bar sections can be used for the post and signal arm bearings the usual sizes are 1/16in tube for the bearing (T116), 5/64in for the main post (T564) and 3/32in for the lower section of the tubular posts (T332). The post cap is a round white metal casting part SC0019 and the lamps are SC0014. For older wooden post signals, use the cast white metal finials. The balance weight and lever are made up from pack SC0041. The spectacle glazing comes in pack code LENS and includes ruby, blue/green and green tints. The 'green' aspect is usually a blue/green shade. When illuminated by the rather yellow flame of the oil lamp, this shows green through the glass. The ladder is S009/3. A fine piece of wire is used to connect the arm to the balance weight and down through the baseboard. Signal posts were generally painted white, with black sections at the bottom and sometimes the top, but CIÉ used aluminium paint on steel posts, giving a silver and black finish. The arm is painted a rather bright shade of red (Humbrol matt blaze No 192 is suitable) with a vertical white line towards the end.

These signals can be made to work easily by various methods. MSE provide a range of different systems. A simple but popular method is the wire-in-tube method. The tube is routed from the edge of the baseboard to the base of the signal. A wire inserted inside the tube is connected to the signal at one end and protrudes from the tube at the other. The operator simply pulls or pushes the wire to operate the signal. A refinement of this mechanical system is to add a miniature lever frame, built up to resemble the frame found in full-sized cabins, with control of the points as well. Alternatively, the signals can be electrically operated, which enables the operator to concentrate all his controls at one place. One way is to use a point solenoid, which can be a little vicious. A good method is something called memory wire. In this system, a special alloy of metal wire is used which has the unusual property of contracting by a percentage of its length when a small electric current is passed through it. When the power is removed, the wire relaxes back to its original length. By making up a small mechanism, this property can be used to operate a crank and, through it, the signal. The motion is quite gentle and smooth and looks fairly realistic. Starter kits for this system are marketed by MSE and C&L Finescale.

From the 1920s, two main changes occurred in British semaphore signalling practice. Three of the four main companies adopted upper quadrant signals, that rose instead of dropped to show clear and all the companies agreed to paint distant arms yellow to distinguish them from the red stop signals. At night distant signals now showed a yellow or green aspect rather than the previous red or green lenses. The Irish Free State had by now been established and thus the GSR did not follow the new British practice in relation to the colour of distant signal arms, though the companies operating in Northern Ireland did conform to the new British practice in relation to distants. The lower quadrant however reigned supreme in Ireland, north and south. The only upper-quadrants in Ireland which most observers can recall were those installed by the LMS/NCC at Larne Harbour.

However, technology was moving on again, and Irish companies did not ignore all developments in signalling engineering. The NCC re-equipped its York Road terminus in Belfast with colour lights, electrically operated points and a 90-lever electro-mechanical frame in 1927, the largest such installation in the British Isles at the time. Meanwhile, the GSR experimented with electro-mechanical lever frames and the remote operation of points by motors and hand-cranked generators to allow the closure of some signal cabins. In the Dublin area, the GSR also introduced colour light signals. These were of two patterns: the familiar two, three or four aspect types and the 'searchlight' or 'theatre-light' design. Instead of the modern traffic light type, with three or four coloured lamps, this had one lamp in the middle of a large disc, containing a rotating system of lenses. This system was installed by the GSR on some of its Dublin suburban lines and was a feature at Amiens Street until electrification of the suburban lines in the 1980s. Irish colour light signals of both the 'searchlight' and multiple two, three and four aspect types are very similar to the British pattern. These are readily available either as kits or ready assembled in the Eckon or Berko ranges. Using LEDs (light-emitting diodes), these signals are easily wired up to multi-position switches. The more unusual colour light configurations, including working theatre board indicators, can be made and supplied to your specifications from specialist companies such as Roger Murray. An article in the *Model Railway News* (July 1956, p166-70) describes how to model searchlight pattern signals using under baseboard light sources. Illumination could probably be achieved more easily now using two or three colour LEDs or fibre-optic cable.

Traditionally, Irish passing stations were signalled for left hand running, with each platform only available for running in one direction. The diagram below shows signalling at a typical GSR passing station on a single line. Approaching from each direction, the driver first meets a distant. In later days, especially on quieter lines where most trains called all stations, some distants were 'fixed' at caution rather than worked from the cabin. This effectively functioned as a speed restriction. In some cases, the GSR used a red chevron on a white board with a lamp on one side as a fixed distant. After the distant comes the home signal, controlling access to the platform or loop. In this example, access to the goods store is rather complex, achieved not by a cross-over off the down loop, but from the up loop involving a diamond crossing. This was common nineteenth century practice, as engineers had a morbid fear of facing points. A facing point is one where an approaching train can run over either route, as opposed to trailing point where there is only one option, and the train must stop and set back to take the other route. Trailing points are safe, as the weight on the wheel flanges will keep the blades firmly in place; facing ones are potentially hazardous due to the risk of the blades shifting under a train and de-railing it. All facing points over which passenger trains run must have a safety device, traditionally a facing point lock, or a plunger that ensures the blades will not move until released from the signal cabin, and a fouling bar, to stop the locks being withdrawn while a train is passing over the turnout. Working point locks are only for the technically minded, but dummy plungers and fouling bars will add a touch of realism. In this layout, both connections to the goods store are by trailing points, which do not strictly need such locking devices. This layout also lacks shunting signals. Here, manoeuvres in and out of the goods yard would be controlled by the shunter giving hand or, at night, lamp signals to the signalman.

In later years, many single line stations were re-arranged to allow each side of the loop to be used by trains in either direction. For example, this was done at Enniscorthy in 1937 and at Kilmacthomas in

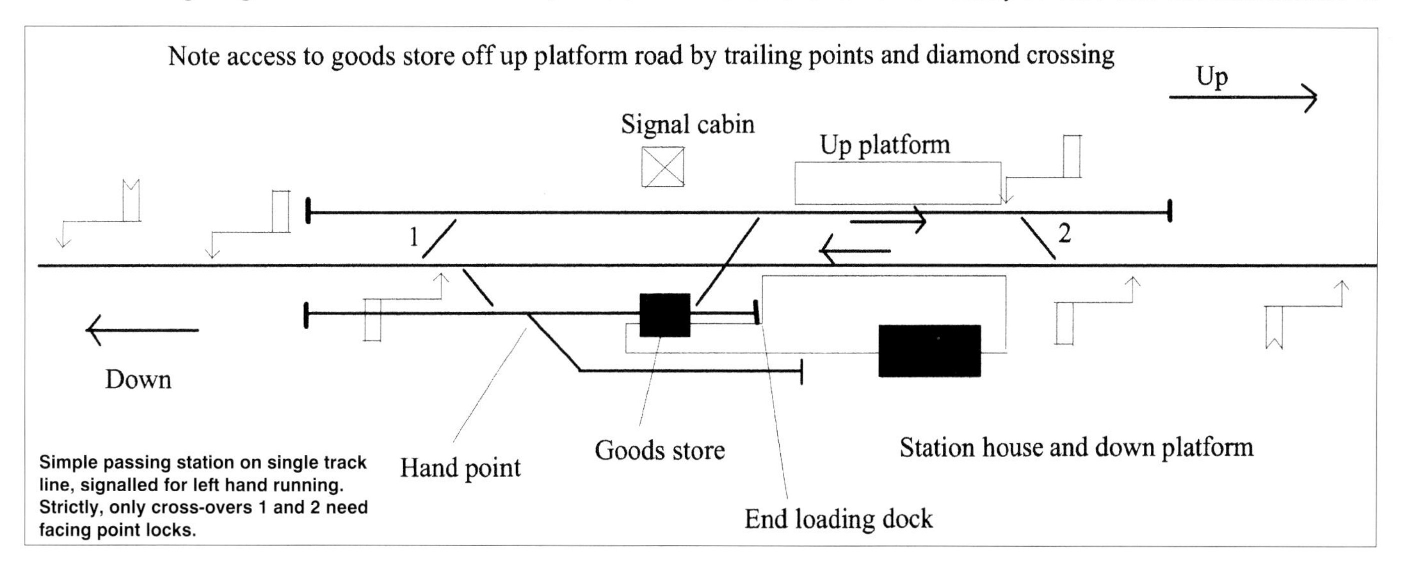

Simple passing station on single track line, signalled for left hand running. Strictly, only cross-overs 1 and 2 need facing point locks.

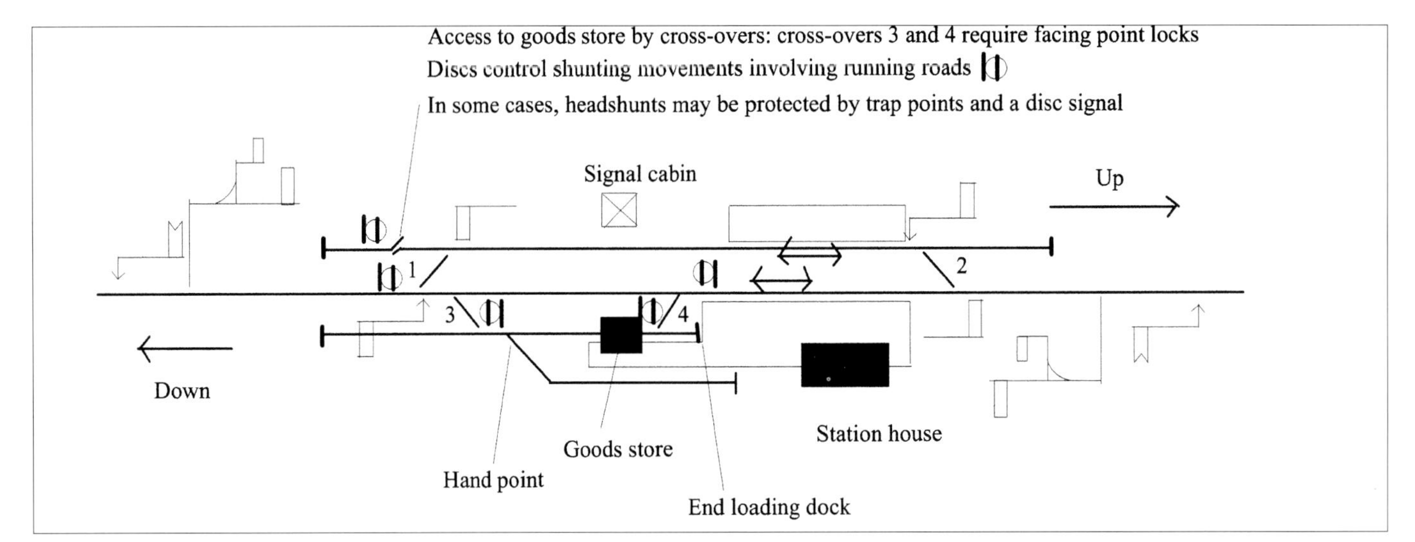

1939. All points off each running road now needed facing point locks, so more complex layouts with diamond crossings tended to become obsolete. Ground signals for shunting were also often added. The diagram above shows our typical wayside station re-signalled for bi-directional running and equipped with shunting discs. Generally, one route allowed 'straight through' running without slowing to negotiate the divergence of a turnout, thus speeding up trains not booked to stop at the station. Another technology to speed up such services was the automatic exchange of ETS tokens, using an arm on the locomotive side and a line-side device to swap the tokens at speed. Lines so equipped include the ex-MGWR line. This technical advance was used to justify the singling of large sections of this line by the GSR whilst not delaying the traffic. This was also used on the NCC main line where some of the fastest schedules ever operated in Ireland with steam traction were introduced in the 1930s. Some of the diesels were fitted up for the system, but it could only be used when there was a second man ('the snatcherman') on the footplate to work the gear. The really technically minded may consider a working model of one of these token exchange devices, but lesser mortals will probably settle for a dummy one at the end of the platform.

Where a train has access to more than one route, such as a branch, bay platform or a passing loop with two-way running, this is often controlled by a bracket signal, the relative height of the main post and the 'doll' and the size of the arms giving some idea of the importance of the two routes. In more modern practice, an illuminated electrical panel may show which route is set, especially at termini with access to several platforms and goods loops. Exit from the station (and usually entry to the next block section) is controlled by the starter at the end of the platform. At some stations on single line sections, as an extra precaution, the starting signal was released by a key on the staff for the section ahead. The signalman could not clear the signal until the section was clear and he could extract a token. At some locations, advanced starting signals were also included, placed further out, permitting shunting, especially where this required access to a cross-over or siding beyond the starter. The most advanced starter controlled entry to the next block section. Other places had outer homes, to allow the signalman to accept a train and hold it if the station was blocked, perhaps by shunting. Elsewhere, 'limit of shunt' boards were provided, usually small cast iron plates at rail level lit by a red lamp, setting a limit to how far trains might set back beyond starting signals without blocking the section. For any movements outside these shunt limits, the signalman had to communicate with the next cabin.

Early railway signalling was mainly concerned with the running lines only, and indeed some quiet locations never got beyond this. But, from the later years of the nineteenth century, engineers devised a whole range of ringed and miniature semaphores, and tilting, rotating or drop-flap ground signals for shunting and freight movements. In more recent years, these have been replaced with small colour light devices. Terminology for these items is rather vague: ground, shunt, subsidiary or disc signals, the latter with scant regard for geometric accuracy. The term 'ground signal' can be rather misleading. To enable these signals to be sighted, they were often mounted on the posts of orthodox semaphores. A common pattern on CIÉ was where a cross-over at the platform end provided access to either the running road (usually controlled by a semaphore) or a siding or locomotive yard (controlled by a 'disc'), as at Castlebar and Nenagh. More rarely, they were carried on brackets from line-side structures, or even their own posts, as at Mullingar. CIÉ nomenclature preferred disc or subsidiary signal, but divided them into 'yellow discs' where a route was available whatever the signal showed, and which could be passed when 'on' with impunity, and red discs, leading to running roads or into trap points. Failing to observe these could result in disciplinary action against the driver. In practice, they are worked by red levers in the cabin, often with one lever releasing two or more discs according to the lie of the points. One particularly thrifty lever in Ennis South cabin used to operate all three discs. This lever normally stood half-way across the frame: pulling it released either of two discs depending on the points. Pushing it back to 'normal' operated the other. Occasionally one lever, painted red and black, operated a disc and a turnout or trap-point together, as at Cahir. The most common mechanical subsidiary signals on IÉ now are rotating discs, with a square and a diamond face; tilting square discs; and round discs. A few older types of shunt signals survived into modern times, such as a rotating one at Thomastown carriage dock and a miniature semaphore at Maynooth.

Where a siding or loop joins a main line by a cross-over, any vehicle running away would run down the headshunt into the stop block. However, where the siding joined the running line by a plain turnout, a runaway wagon could get out on the main line, if its weight was enough to close the point blades. Such sidings should be protected by trap points which in Ireland were often no more than a single movable blade on the off side rail, positioned to throw the vehicle clear of the road. Trap points should not be confused with catch points. These were most often found on inclines. A train running in the correct direction would pass over these without incident, but they would de-rail any breakways running down the incline. Working traps are not really necessary in the smaller scales, but dummy ones, made by filing and soldering a small length of rail in place, add a touch of realism.

Levers in Irish cabins are painted according to function: red for stop signals (and shunting discs), green for distants (unlike the English practice of yellow), black for points, dark-blue for point locks (bands of blue and black for levers which both release the locks and reverse the points), brown for stops on level crossing and wicket gates, white for spare or disconnected levers. Away from stations, distants were often used to protect level crossing gates, from one or sometimes both directions, according to the visibility of the gates and their lamps. Such signals were either operated from small groundframes at the keepers' cottages, or sometimes moved by wires attached to the gate heels, such that opening and closing the gates automatically set the signals. Incidentally, visibility often dictated the position or height of semaphore posts, and sometimes a white board, called a sighting board, was fixed behind the arm, or a patch of masonry on bridges behind a signal was whitewashed. Some signals were suspended from gallows or perched on brackets to improve sighting. One solution used at Portarlington, where the down starter was obscured by a bridge, was to use an extremely tall post with a second repeater arm visible above the bridge. Modern operation of level crossings involves replacing the gates with lifting barriers and protection by colour light signals. In some cases, operation is automatic, the opening and closing of the gates being initiated by treadles or other sensors on each side of the crossing, which are activated by the wheel flanges of an approaching train.

The GNR(I) had its own characteristic lower quadrant semaphores, with rather short arms, on square posts, but latterly as an economy measure, hung on creosoted telegraph poles. The BCDR used its own automatic signalling on the Bangor line, and the BNCR followed the practice of the English Great Northern in using somersault signals where a complex crank arrangement flipped the arm from horizontal to vertical, with the spectacle glass bearing the lenses completely separate. With a few LNWR type lower quadrants on the Larne line, the upper quadrants at the harbour, a fine display of GNR(I) brackets at Lisburn and lattice post starters at Bangor, NIR still had a fascinating variety of signals in the mid 1980s. With the exception of Castlerock and Portrush, the whole network is now equipped with modern colour light signalling. On IÉ, despite the steady extension of the CTC area since the 1980s, there are still extensive sections controlled by traditional semaphores and ETS. For some years, CIÉ/IÉ signal arms have been painted a sort of Day-Glo high visibility orange, or plastic overlays have been used on older wooden arms, rather than the usual red pigment, which sometimes weathers rather pink. In the last few years, visibility has been further improved by adding an even brighter band to the outer ends of the semaphore arms.

How you run your model is of course a matter of personal taste. You can simply marshal, shunt and run trains as you wish. But, many modellers prefer to give some rhyme and reason to the sequence of events on their layouts, by drawing up a timetable. The late Sam Carse built an extensive model of his beloved Donegal narrow gauge, with a working timetable, using a compressed schedule, with a day's activity spread over about 90 minutes and a speeded up clock for shunting! Most modellers just use the timetable as a sequence, rather than scaling time, and at many Irish wayside stations, such an approach would generate long quiet periods! Here, access to working timetables and weekly circulars will give you a feel for the prototype service, or for a freelance line, some idea of the frequency of trains. You can use some random system (such as throwing dice or drawing playing cards) to decide the unknowns: how many wagons on each goods working or whether passenger trains will convey non-passenger stock like horse boxes. Wagons can be colour coded by small removable tags, and daily casting of dice decides if they move (and if so in which direction), or stay put. You can assign maximum loads to certain goods trains, designing your system such that occasionally these will be exceeded, requiring another working to run mixed, or an 'overload special'. Modern image modellers can use such random systems to determine if cement and fertiliser trains operate.

As regards train formation, some books contain detailed information about which vehicles appeared on specific services; the other option is to study period photographs. Until the 1960s, Irish trains tended to be rather glorious mixes of rolling stock of all sorts of eras, designs and profiles, with many passenger services containing arc, clerestory and elliptical roofed stock and many included six-wheelers. Only the main line expresses showed uniformity, such as the modern steel flush sided sets used on the GNR(I) Dublin-Belfast expresses or the GSR Cork Day Mails. Each section had maximum loads, depending on gradients and locomotive class. These are unlikely to be exceeded by modellers, with limited space, but some routes had more stringent rules, such as forbidding vehicles with passengers (except for grooms in horseboxes!) being attached behind the rear van, or banning coaches with less than 18in diameter buffer heads on the Valencia branch. For mixed trains, extra rules pertained. On the GSR, vehicles containing passengers had to be at the front, their continuous brakes connected to the engine, with a goods brake at the tail. As far as possible, these trains had to observe station stops at least every 10 miles. The load for mixed trains was 30 vehicles, although this was further limited to 10 wagons for a 10-ton goods brakevan, 13 wagons for a 12-ton, and 20 for a 16-ton van.

Below: **A disused GSR pattern rotating shunt signal, at Greystones in 1984.** Alan O'Rourke

Above left: **An example of a GSR/CIÉ lower quadrant signal mounted on a steel post was recorded at Roscrea, in 1991.**

Above centre: **This bracket version of the tubular post design signals trains from Westport arriving at Claremorris. The abandoned 'Burma Road' to Collooney is to the left of this 1992 view.**

Above right: **Some railway companies, particularly in Scotland, were very fond of iron lattice posts for signals. A few Irish companies like the DSER followed suit, and this specimen is one of the starters at Arklow, seen in 1996.**

Bottom left: **These BNCR somersault signals were still in use in 1984. The one on the left in the off position shows how the arm and spectacle plate are independently pivoted.**

Bottom right: **Standard GSWR /GSR lower quadrant home signal on wooden post, at Roscrea.** All photographs on this page, Alan O'Rourke

Right: **This is an example of a smaller station, which is not a block post but which has retained its signal cabin to control a set of level crossing gates. This view of Castleconnel, on the Limerick to Ballybrophy line, looking north, was taken in 1991. The semaphore home arm indicates the position of the station gates, the distant arm below relates to the next crossing up the line.** Alan O'Rourke

Below: **A CIÉ liveried Woolwich Mogul No 395 passes the starter signals at Adavoyle Junction. The signals are accurate models of GNR(I) prototypes on wooden posts which taper upwards.** Tony Wright, courtesy British Railway Modelling

CLIFFONEY STATION CABIN

Photographs on the opposite page:

Top: **This model of Manorhamilton signal cabin on the SLNCR, in 7mm scale, was built from an Alphagraphix card kit. The prototype was a standard Saxby & Farmer design. The upper part of the structure was very similar to boxes supplied to English lines such as the LBSCR. The use of a stone built base is more typical of Irish practice.** Roger Crombleholme

Bottom left: **The cabin at Roscrea was a typical GSWR type built to the design of the Railway Signal Company. The frame at Roscrea contained 24 levers.** Alan O'Rourke

Bottom right: **This 4mm scale model of a MGWR cabin, made by David Malone, was based on the one at Dromod on the Dublin to Sligo line.** David Malone

Photographs on this page:

Right: **This drawing showing details of GSWR and CIÉ semaphores and ground signals was produced by David Malone.**

Below: **Another view of Tony Miles' peerless Adavoyle Junction layout. Blue liveried GNR 'U' class 4-4-0 No 204 *Antrim* approaches Adavoyle Junction station with a goods train. The starting signals are to the left whilst the impressive gantry can be seen in the distance.** Tony Wright, courtesy British Railway Modelling

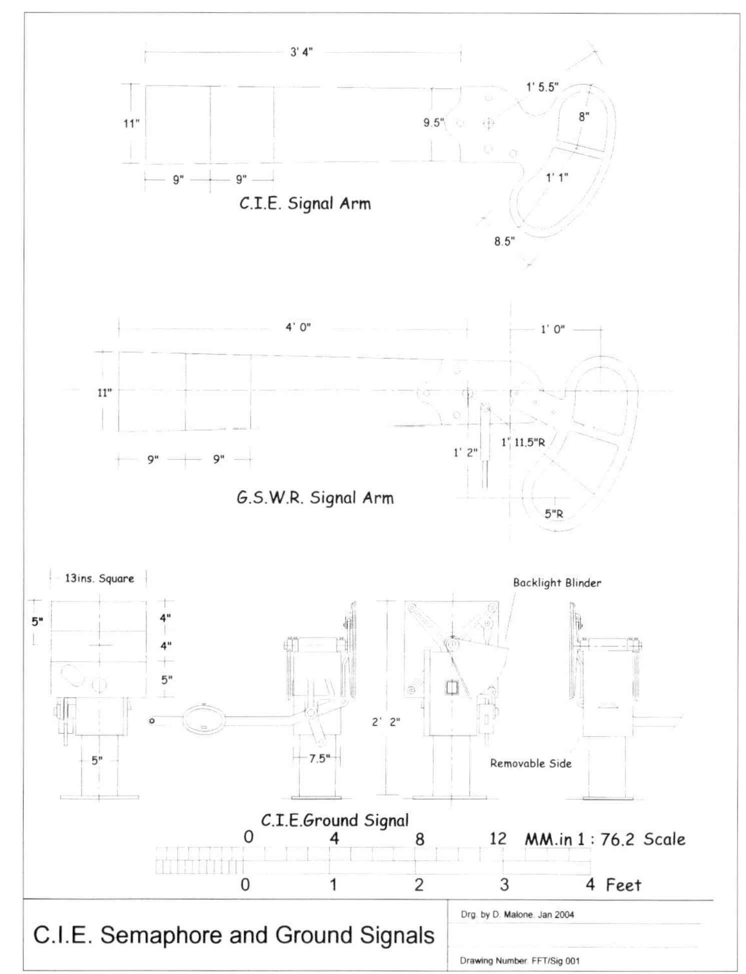

CHAPTER 6

THE NARROW GAUGE

From the 1960s, the availability of TT (12mm gauge) track and mechanisms encouraged modellers like the late David Lloyd to create Irish narrow gauge layouts in 4mm scale. David returned to Irish narrow gauge 20 years later, after living in West Cork, and set out to build an atmospheric recreation of a railway might-have-been, if certain ambitious 19th century schemes had come to fruition. The plan included 30-odd static but highly detailed models of narrow gauge locomotives, such as the West Clare 0-6-2Ts, the Cavan & Leitrim's 0-6-4T No 9 *King Edward* and the Clogher Valley Railway 2-6-2T No 4. He produced not only his models but an excellent book of locomotive drawings to inspire others, though sadly, David died before completing this work. Other modellers like Sam Carse, used scales of either 5mm, 5.5mm or 6mm to the foot with OO gauge track, wheels and mechanisms to represent the 3ft gauge, and some modellers were using such combinations to recreate the CDR as far back as 1948. Another pioneer was George Hanan who built 16.5mm gauge, 5mm scale models of the CDR system (see *Railway Modeller* July 1959 and March 1963).

More recent approaches include 7mm finescale on 21mm gauge, and some modellers have adopted the compromise of 7mm models on 16.5mm track (technically 2ft 4in) for Irish models, allowing the use of commercial mechanisms, such as C&L 4-4-0Ts on the Tri-ang 'L1' chassis (with extra motion from Tri-ang spares), Tralee & Dingle 2-6-0Ts based on the Tri-ang 'Transcontinental' 4-6-4T and six-coupled mechanisms, hidden under the convenient skirts of a CVR engine, built using filed down CCW boiler fittings.

Going in the opposite direction, several modellers have used 3mm scale and 9mm gauge for 3ft models, such as Paul Windle (*Model Railways*, May 1992) and Charles Insley (*Railway Modeller*, June 2003). Potential models using commercial components in this scale include T&D Hunslet 2-6-0Ts (Minitrix 2-6-2 chassis, GEM TT '14XX' chimney and other boiler fittings from the Golden Arrow Southwold Railway locomotive kits); C&L 4-4-0Ts (on a Graham Farish '2P' chassis); T&D Kerr Stuart 2-6-0Ts (on a Farish '08' chassis); a West Clare section railcar on modified Ro-Co centre cab 0-6-0 diesel shunter and Egger-Bahn railcar bogie and a West Clare diesel locomotive built on a modified Arnold DB Bo-Bo chassis, with coaches running on Lima bogies with 6mm diameter spoked wheels from the Dundas Models range. Such modellers use track like Peco code 55 finescale N gauge. One modeller has made an NCC 'S' class 2-4-2T in 3mm scale using the Farish '4P' chassis, fitted with pony trucks from the same company's GWR Prairie tank fore and aft. The lack of a proper footplate complicates making the superstructure, and the best approach seems to be to make the tank/cab unit as a box, hanging the rear footplate, bearing cab back-sheet and buffer beam off this, and mounting the front footplate on the cylinder block, with the cylinder wrappers as downward extensions of the tank-sides. Remember that being a compound, the cylinders are of unequal diameters! The Walschaerts valve gear will probably need simplifying on the model. A few modellers are even exploring modelling the 3ft lines in 2mm scale, an option here being the use of Z gauge mechanisms, the gauge of 6.5mm being close enough.

A number of modellers have built up economic fleets of rolling stock by judicious use of old and now second hand Tri-ang TT components, such as using motor bogies from the A1A diesel for County Donegal railcars, with card superstructure; a Castle chassis for CDR class 4 4-6-0Ts; 'reversed' pacific mechanisms for CDR 2-6-4T; Jinties for CVR 0-4-2Ts or NCC Beyer-Peacock 0-6-0Ts; and a die-cast

Left: **The passenger station and footbridge of Andy Cundick's OOn3 model of the CDR's Donegal Town station. Railcars Nos 20 and 8 are at the platforms.** Andy Cundick

Right: **Another view of Andy Cundick's OOn3 model of Donegal Town with a railcar passing the CDR's only diesel locomotive, No 11 *Phoenix*.** Andy Cundick

Below right: **This model of CVR No 6 *Erne* in 4mm scale is running on a Berliner-Bahnen TT 0-4-0T chassis. The side skirts hide the lack of a trailing axle. The body is made from Plasticard with commercially available boiler fittings added. The lettering is made from transfers intended to be used for pre-war models of English Southern Railway locomotives! This font was very close to that used by the CVR.** Alan O'Rourke

wagon chassis for a variety of goods vehicles. The County Donegal wagon fleet included a number of tank wagons, and the Shell ones can be adapted from old Tri-ang TT tank wagons and the British Petroleum ones from the Ertl 'Thomas the Tank Engine' series tar or milk tanks, mounted on Ninelines Donegal wagon chassis. However, it is now many years since the Tri-ang TT range was in production and models are only available second hand. Compared to modern ranges, the track and wheel standards are very coarse, and mechanisms will by now need new motors and wheels.

Recently, Peco have introduced a range of 12mm gauge track and pointwork, based on continental metre gauge practice, but quite suitable for Irish and Isle of Man 3ft gauge in 4mm scale. TT gauge is still made on the continent, as is a certain amount of 12mm gauge equipment in HO scale for metre gauge prototypes (marketed as HOm scale). Much of this, such as Tillig and Bemo, is rather expensive for kit-bashing, but the Berliner-Bahnen range, especially if you can pick it up second hand, provides some chassis and mechanisms including 20mm wheelbase coach bogies, 17mm freight bogies and six-wheel coach underframes, with the middle axle arranged with generous side pay for sharp curves. The Berliner-Bahnen range includes an 0-6-0 diesel chassis, which can be hidden under any locomotive with tramway-type skirts, and a 2-6-2 tender engine, with 17mm + 17mm coupled wheelbase which, with slight modification, suits the West Clare 2-6-2Ts, if one can tolerate having the cylinders too far back. There is also a 2-8-0 locomotive. The chassis of this could be used for one of the LLSR's big 4-8-0s, although the modeller will have to accept a fair degree of compromise in terms of wheelbase and driving wheel diameter. (Backwoods Miniatures has produced more accurate etched brass kits for the big Swilly eight-coupled engines, but at present only the 4-8-0 is listed as in production.) A couple of eight-coupled tanks are also listed, and with somewhat more drastic surgery the wheelbase is not too far off the Castlederg & Victoria Bridge Tramway's 2-6-0T, although it is probably easier to model this locomotive on this chassis after its re-construction to a 2-6-2T by the Clogher Valley with more overhang at the rear. Incidentally, continental TT is different to British. As in OO and to a lesser extent N, British manufacturers tend to round up scales, so that the gauge is too narrow, which has certain advantages for getting train sets to go round sharp bends. British TT was probably the worst culprit, with a ratio of 1:100, and a scale gauge of only 4ft! Continental manufacturers used a more appropriate ratio of 1:120, giving the correct gauge for 12mm track representing 4ft 8½in.

Was the Listowel & Ballybunion monorail narrow gauge or no gauge? All its stock sat astride the 'A' girders that carried the track. Despite closing in 1924, the line has attracted several modellers, including Fry in 7mm (see *Model Railway News*, November 1968). Solutions to this unusual prototype include designing special jigs for the trackwork, using the guide-rails lower down the 'A' frames for pick-ups, and curved turntables instead of points, with grooved rather than flanged wheels running along the actual mono-rail and spur gears on an axle to these wheels providing the motive power. In 4mm, a simpler alternative is to solder flat-bottomed running rail to the top of steel pins driven

Above: **These models of two ex-Tralee & Dingle bogie vehicles have been built from Alphagraphix card kits. Both are shown as running on the C&L section of CIÉ in that company's green livery. The little signal cabin in the background, based on a Londonderry & Lough Swilly Railway prototype, is another Alphagraphix kit.** Alan O'Rourke

diagonally into a wood or fibre sleeper base, with the guide rails, lower down on the pins, of piano wire, soldered in place using a jig. The 4mm locomotive had the motor mounted in one half of the tender, with worm and gear transmission across the chassis to spur gears on the opposite side of the centre-line, the spur driving pulley wheels along the mono-rail. In the smaller scale, knurled rather than smooth pulley wheels may be needed for adequate adhesion. The chassis also carried two thin silver steel guides, one insulated from the chassis and weighted to cause the vehicles all to lean slightly to one side, the second silver steel guide acting as a counter-balance to prevent the stock swinging off the running rail. Power was delivered by having all the 'A' frame and the running rail positive, with the guides as pick-ups (see *Model Railway News*, February. 1962). Alphagraphix now make card kits for a Listowel & Ballybunion train in 7mm scale. Other useful articles on modelling the Ballybunion monorail appeared in *Model Railways* October 1971 and *Model Railway News* September 1968.

As usual, the greatest commercial support is in 4mm scale. Many of these kits are designed to run on either 9mm track or 12mm. The more popular combination is 9 mm (009 in 4mm) using N gauge mechanisms. These are intended mainly for models of Welsh narrow gauge lines with gauges of about 2ft, but many of the Irish prototypes provide variety for freelance modellers in that scale, while the added sales make such runs more commercially viable. However, the bigger Swilly and Donegal stock would dwarf anything from the Welsh lines. 12mm gauge on 4mm scale (OOn3) is of course spot on for the 3ft lines from Ireland. It also suits the Isle of Man's railways, which have attracted some commercial support over the years. Producing plastic and white metal kits in other scales means making new moulds, and so is prohibitively expensive, but with modern technology, the artwork for etched brass kits can be scaled up or down more easily, making it practical to produce the same kit in several scales. A good example of this is the Worsley Works range of etched brass Irish narrow gauge locomotives and carriages in 3mm, 4mm, 5.5mm and 7mm scales. These are marketed as 'scratch-aids', so the kits comprise just body etches and choice of running gear and other fittings is left to the builder. Some interesting items appear such as the CIÉ 'F' class 0-4-0+0-4-0 diesel locomotive built for the West Clare section. The body makes up easily but the chassis is a little trickier. The Worsley range of carriages for the Irish narrow gauge is now very extensive, including stock from the CDR, T&D, C&L, L&LS, WCR, the NCC lines, the Giant's Causeway Tramway and the Letterkenny & Burtonport Extension Railway. The company also makes bogies, kits for the Cleminson chassis for six-wheelers and components for CDR wagon chassis. Three more CDR coaches, the Oldbury panelled Composite and matchboarded Third and Brake third, are available in kits as a three-pack from Backwoods. Branchlines make etched kits for the T&D matchboard-sided Third, and CVR coaches and horse box. Chivers Finelines at one stage made an etched brass kit in 4mm scale for the T&D horse box. Further Donegal coaches can be adapted from cut down moulded sides from the Ratio kits for MR suburban stock.

The following locomotive and railcar kits, listed below by operator, are available at present or have been in production in recent years in 4mm scale:

LLSR/LBER: 4-8-0 and 4-8-4T from Backwoods Miniatures; Kerr Stuart 4-6-2T from Worsley; Andrew Barclay 4-6-0T from Worsley.

CDR/CVR: Atkinson Walker steam tractor (later CDR No 11 *Phoenix*) from Backwoods Miniatures.

CDR: Class 5 2-6-4T from Backwoods Miniatures (Worsley market a conversion pack to modify this to the Class 5a); Railcars 4, 7, 8, 10 (ex-CVR), 12, 14 from Backwoods.

C&LR: 4-4-0T from Backwoods Miniatures.

CVR: 0-4-2T from Backwoods Miniatures.

T&DR: 2-6-0T from Branchlines.

Ballymena & Larne/NCC: 2-4-0T. The Branchlines kit of the first series Isle of Man Beyer-Peacock 2-4-0Ts is very close to the two engines of this wheel arrangement supplied to the Ballymena & Larne, the main differences being different-sized side tanks.

Anbrico used to produce a white metal kit of Donegal railcars Nos 19 and 20, which still survive on the Isle of Man. The West Clare section had some similar railcars. These old kits occasionally turn up at swap-meets and can usually be made to work again with a little time and effort. Tra-

Left: **Although not often modelled, Bord na Móna's industrial narrow gauge lines can offer some interesting prototypes. This 4mm scratch-built railcar has a Plasticard body and runs on a modified Farish HST motor bogie. The axles were simply changed for longer ones suitable for 12mm track.** Stephen Johnson

Below left: **Among some of the more unusual Bord na Móna prototypes are their rail tractors. A Ferguson tractor, with its cab rebuilt, is mounted on a skip chassis with a chain drive fitted from the tractor's rear axle to the rail wheels. The model of the tractor is too small to be motorised and is pushed along by the powered personnel carrier behind it. This vehicle, the original made from corrugated iron, is based on one which ran on the Bord na Móna system at Glenties in County Donegal.** Stephen Johnson

malan make kits for the Kitson and Wilkinson steam trams, which can be used for models of the Portstewart, Dublin & Lucan and Giant's Causeway tramways. The same company used to make a conversion kit to build Hill of Howth No 10 from the Tower Model SHMD tram. The Tramalan double deck trailer car is also suitable for Portstewart vehicles and, with modifications, for the Lucan single decker. For motorising railcar kits, suitable 12mm gauge motor bogies are the LH or Halling bogies (23, 27 or 31mm wheelbase) from the Model Tramway Shop, 18 Glanffrwd Road, Glynhir, Pontarddulais, Swansea SA4 8QE, or the 5.5mm Association bogie (22mm wheelbase) from Mike Chinney, Pennant, Upper Downing Road, Whitford, Holywell, Flintshire CH8 9AJ.

A number of narrow gauge white metal and moulded plastic wagon kits are also available from Parkside Dundas, Ninelines and Backwoods Miniatures. The Ninelines kit for the English Southwold Railway open wagons can be modified to represent the Cork & Muskerry ballast wagons. The Ratio kit for the GWR open-C wagon can be used for one of the CDR's bogie open wagons if the ends are narrowed by 4mm and 4ft 3in Worsley bogies are fitted.

For buildings, there is a wide range of card kits from Alphagraphix. In addition to 4mm scale card rolling stock, that company also markets the Tyrconnel range of cast resin/white metal kits for 7mm scale Irish narrow gauge subjects and has recently negotiated with Slaters to provide wheels for 21mm gauge for these kits.

A good example of a high quality finescale Irish narrow gauge model, making good use of the locomotive and rolling stock kits now on the market, is the Chester Model Railway Club's Dingle layout, which appeared in the December 2002 and January and February 2003 issues of *Railway Modeller*.

For something different, Bord na Móna, the Irish peat company, has an extensive industrial railway system of nearly 1,000 miles of track with some 350 locomotives still operating today. Some of these lines are very near to, or cross, existing IÉ lines. Bord na Móna use the 3ft gauge, although some 2ft gauge systems were also in use. Of these, only the Glenties system in County Donegal still survives, as a worker owned co-operative. The locomotive stock ranges from standard design Ruston & Hornsby 48DLs through to Simplex, Deutz and Gliesmac locomotives. In recent years, specially designed Hunslet types have been produced, notably the *Wagonmaster* and DH type. Early operations concentrated on sod peat transported in four-wheel open framework wagons with bogie wagons later being used as well. Today, milled peat is extracted and transported in alloy sided bogie wagons. Nothing is available in 4mm scale but a *Wagonmaster* is produced in a larger scale (16mm:1ft) by Essel Engineering and a Ruston & Hornsby type is also available in 7mm scale. Those modelling in 4mm scale will have to scratch-build all of the stock, but this is not as difficult as it may seem. Kean-Maygib will supply suitable 3 hole disc wheels for 12mm track that can be used for the bogie wagons. N gauge bogie diamond frames from the Farish range are very close to those used by Bord na Móna and a little surgery can produce suitable bogies. A scratch-built Plasticard body is easily constructed. Locomotives are more difficult, requiring the modeller to scratch-build the body at least. Commercially available 12mm gauge motor bogies from the 3SMR range can be used to good effect in a model for a Hunslet DH or Gliesmac for instance. Locomotives using inside frames and connecting rods, such as the *Wagonmasters* or Deutz types would require a scratchbuilt chassis. Among the other unusual vehicles are the railcars. These vehicles resemble a self-propelled caravan and can been seen at all Bord na Móna sites. One solution here has been to scratch-build the body and mount on a re-gauged Farish N gauge HST power bogie. Modelling Bord na Móna can offer the modeller an unusual take on Irish railways, especially if the peat extraction machinery is included, as some of it looks as if designed by W Heath-Robinson.

Some modellers combine the hobbies of gardening and railways, building outdoor narrow gauge lines in the larger scales, sometimes with live steam. These tend to be quite 'chunky' with a good deal of metal and timber in the construction, and mark the transition from railway modelling to miniature engineering, and builders must be prepared to invest time in proper civil engineering and track foundations, if the permanent way is not to deteriorate rapidly in the battle with the elements, moles and other wildlife. Even a modest garden will give you a lot more room for your railway, allowing scale radius curves and station platform lengths, while creating the impression of a railway that is actually going somewhere. Working in the garden allows you to enjoy the changing seasons, weather and foliage, and can produce wonderfully atmospheric operation, as described by Neil Ramsay who works in 15mm scale on 45mm gauge: 'To watch your own six-foot long rake of tatty mixed Irish stock trundling through real scenery in the dappled sunlight, at a scale 15mph and with a cloud of steam hanging in the air– well, it is worth every penny.'

Some modellers have produced successful small scale outdoor layouts, but the larger scales are easier and look better. There are three obvious choices. The first is 10mm to the foot on 32mm (O gauge) track. This is big enough for live steam, but also suitable for electric operation, either via the track or using batteries. It is also small enough for you to be able to create a real impression of distance. As a 'standard' scale but on a narrower gauge, many useful parts are available off the shelf either in 10mm scale or by judicious use of conventional O gauge components such as chassis and wheels.

A second option is 16mm to the foot on 45mm (gauge one) track. The use of 16mm to the foot on 32mm track is very popular with narrow gauge railway modellers in the UK working on models of 2ft gauge prototypes. This is a good scale for modelling in the garden, with reliable and controllable live steam locomotives, and large chunky rolling stock. With the popularity and availability of LGB and Bachmann G scale products, many narrow gauge garden railway modellers are now modelling 16mm scale (or thereabouts) on 45mm track, giving a reasonably close approximation to the 3ft gauge. The advantage of 16mm scale is that there is a wide variety of parts, kits and off the shelf products that can be used as the basis of Irish models. For example, kits of Welshpool & Llanfair Railway stock can be used as the basis for Irish goods vehicles.

The third option is 15mm to the foot on 45mm track. In some ways this is the ideal large scale for Irish narrow gauge, giving the perfect scale-gauge relationship. It is increasing in popularity in the USA, where it is seen as a correct scale alternative to G scale for modelling American 3ft gauge prototypes, but so far has a very limited following in Europe.

Although very little Irish stock is available off the shelf, scratch-building in the larger scales is really straightforward, as everything is so much easier to handle (and see!). Rolling stock can be fabricated from wood, usually ply and strip wood as supplied for aero and boat modellers, plastic, brass or even cardboard, and you can add as much or as little detail as you want. In both 10mm and 16mm scales there are plenty of suitable components commercially available including wheels, bogies and couplings. In 15mm scale the choice is much more limited, but as the scales are so close, 16mm parts are often equally suitable: a difference of 40mm on the length of a coach is significant, but less than 1mm on a lamp top or chopper coupling is just not noticeable.

Below: **This 4mm scale model of a CDR Lavatory composite was built from plywood using drawings by the late Sam Carse, which were published in *Model Railways* in 1976. The carriage runs on Berliner-Bahnen bogies. Worsley Works now offers an etched brass body kit for this vehicle.** Alan O'Rourke

Top right: **This 7mm scale model of the LBER'S solitary horse box was built from an Alphagraphix card body kit. It runs on a composite white metal and resin chassis supplied by the same company.** Roger Crombleholme

Below right: **West Clare Railway 2-6-2T No 9 *Fergus*, in 4mm scale. The model is built of Plasticard with boiler fittings adapted from commercial turnings and castings, following the drawings in David Lloyd's book, and runs on a slightly modified Berliner-Bahnen TT chassis. This is not quite right as the cylinders should be further forward, but the overall impression still capture, the rather brick-like squareness of these engines.** Alan O'Rourke

There are a number of options for motive power. Electric G-scale chassis, or the O gauge equivalents, are a good basis for Irish 3ft locomotives. They are well built and powerful, and can be easily converted from track power to battery operation. With a body scratch-built in styrene or brass, a very convincing Irish locomotive can be made. Diesel railcars can also be scratch-built using a proprietary electric chassis as the power units. All those Donegal railcars make fine models, though they can be a bit difficult to construct, but you can always start with the more box-like shape of a West Clare Drewry railcar.

Live steam is more practical outdoors than in smaller scale indoor layouts, and is the big attraction of modelling in the garden. However, unless you have the workshop facilities and engineering skills to produce your own engines, a finished locomotive will now cost the best part of £1,000. In 16mm scale there is a wide variety of efficient and controllable narrow gauge prototypes available. Powered by butane gas, meths or occasionally coal, and often radio controlled, they are safe, easy to run and very reliable. Unfortunately Irish prototypes are few and far between, but some of the freelance and other narrow gauge models can, with the addition of a few details, be made to look a bit more Irish. The Roundhouse Campbeltown & Machrihanish locomotive for example has the size and feel of an Irish 3ft gauge machine. Occasionally it is possible to find that one of the smaller manufactures such as Archangel Models, has produced a batch of real Irish locomotives, such as the Stephenson-built Cavan & Leitrim 4-4-0Ts, or the Ballymena & Larne Railway's Beyer, Peacock 2-4-0T, modified from their Isle of Man prototype, by DJB Engineering. Over the years, various Irish large scale models have been marketed, including LLSR 4-6-2Ts, the T&D's first No 4, an 0-4-2T tramway type locomotive used on the Castlegregory branch and examples of that line's 2-6-0 and 2-6-2 tanks. To run with these Tenmille had a TDR cattle wagon. Archangel Models produced an 0-4-0 tram engine from the Giant's Causeway line and John Campbell produced a model of the LLSR 4-8-0. As mentioned earlier the Bord na Móna *Wagonmaster* was sold by Essel Engineering and Brandbright made models of the the CVR Atkinson Walker railcar and rail-lorry. These models have been made to either 15 or 16mm to the foot scale but if you are a competent model engineer, you can build your own locomotive. A good way to start is to buy a proprietary chassis and boiler and scratch-build a brass body to go with these.

Brass or nickel silver rail will last forever outside, and you can either buy the ready-made plastic sleepered variety, or make your own, such as using flat-bottomed brass track pinned in prototypical fashion to widely spaced wooden sleepers. The brass soon weathers to a convincing dull brown colour. Plastic ready-made track is robust and easy to lay, and both look even more realistic when ballasted. A few line-side details such as signals and buildings really help to set the scene in the garden though even the most modest of buildings can be quite large in these scales. If left out all year, expect to do regular maintenance. Luckily, most Irish narrow gauge lines require relatively few such line-side details.

It is much easier to run and operate a garden railway if it is raised off the ground. Ground level lines can really look fantastic with suitable planting, but you do spend a lot of time looking down on the roofs, and suffer more from leaves and other debris with consequent derailments. Lifting the track onto waist high baseboards is easier on the back, but you tend to lose the scenic aspects. The ideal solution is a raised bank or rockery, though building this can take a lot of hard work. Another option is to join one of the garden railway societies and try to visit a few local lines before you start upon your own programme of hefty civil engineering.

For those interested in larger scale narrow gauge modelling, there is now an active on-line group, 1 to 20.3 Irish and Manx Narrow Gauge (that is, 15mm:1ft scale), although the postings also include much useful information on large scale and outdoor narrow gauge modelling in general. The relevant web address is: http://groups.yahoo.com/group/oneto20point3IrishNG/

Above: **One of wagons most frequently seen on the Bord na Móna systems is the bogie milled peat wagon. The body can easily be made from Plasticard sheet with additional strips of the same material used to model the metal reinforcement bars on the outside of the wagon. The bogies are a modified version of those used on the Farish container flat wagon. These are fitted with 12mm axles and Kean-Maygib wheels. The wagon's load of milled peat is modelled using some of Woodland Scenics dark earth flock, or you could even get some of the real thing from the greenhouse!** Stephen Johnson

Left: **This 14mm scale model of a Tralee & Dingle coach has been built for outdoor use on a garden railway.** Ken Elliot

Top right: **This 14mm scale model of a West Clare Railway open cattle wagon was built from plywood with commercial components used for its running gear.**

Below: **A short train of Irish narrow gauge stock on Ken Elliot's garden railway headed by a battery powered steam outline locomotive.**

Bottom: **A model of one of the West Clare Railway's six-wheel goods brake vans brings up the tail of a goods train.**
All photographs on this page, Ken Elliot

Above: **This 4mm scale model of the LBER bogie brake van No 7 was built from plywood and runs on modified Berliner-Bahnen bogies.** Alan O'Rourke

Below: **This all metal model of a Bord na Móna *Wagonmaster* is made by Essel Engineering, in 16mm scale, to run on the technically too narrow O gauge track. A version of this model was also produced to run on 45mm gauge track. The battery powered motor drives a jack shaft under the cab with rod transmission thence to the wheels.** Ian Lawrence

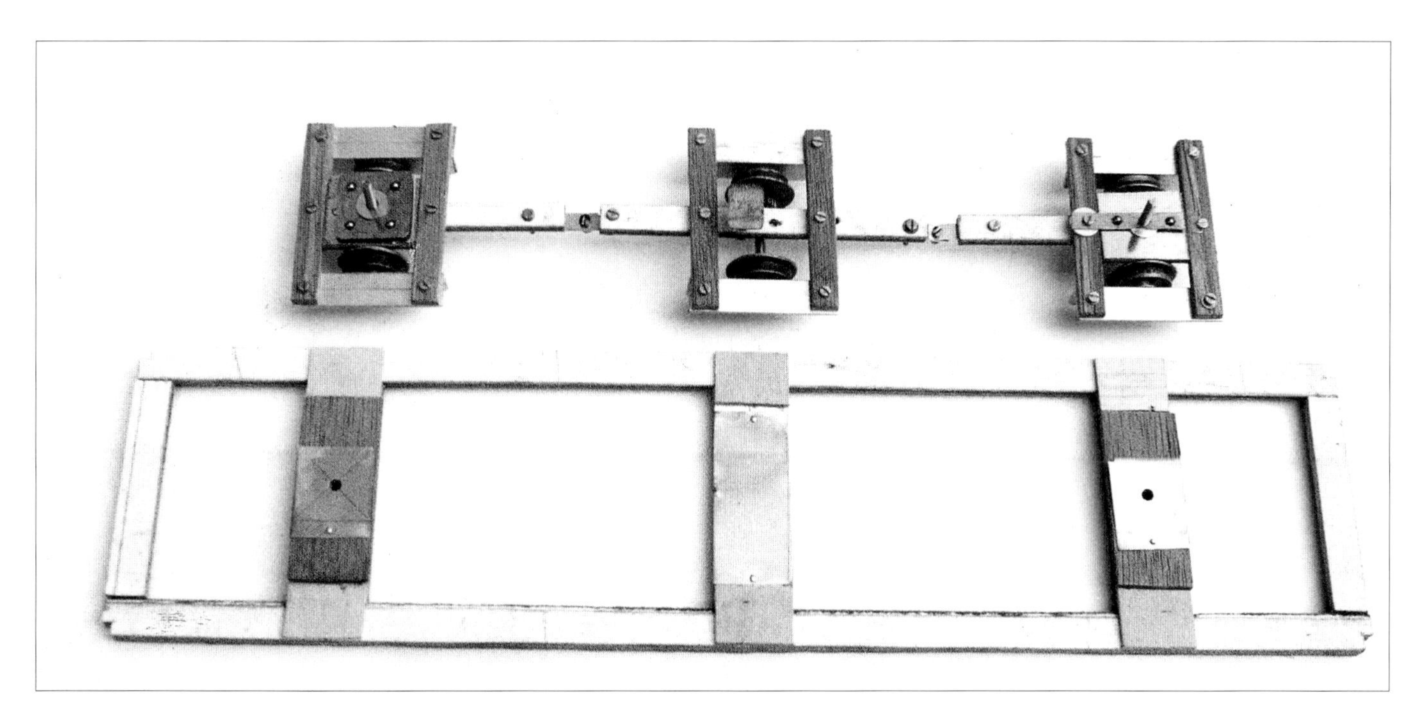

Above: **This view shows the underframe of the WCR goods brake van, seen running on page 57, under construction and the Cleminson chassis used on the vehicle which allows the centre wheels to move sideways. This was useful both on the prototype and on the model to allow tight curves to be negotiated. In the manufacture of the chassis ½in alloy angle section is used for the axle carriers, with small ball and socket joints and a sprung shoe to keep the centre axle on the track.** Ken Elliot

Below: **A general view of Andy Cundick's OOn3 model of the CDR's Donegal Town station with railcars Nos 14 and 8 at the platforms.** Andy Cundick

CASTLEFINN

Opposite page, top: **Two further views of Andy Cundick's splendid recreation of the CDR. Two railcars and an assortment of goods stock are seen at Donegal Town station. The main buildings are still in place and today are occupied by the County Donegal Railway Restoration Society who have preserved many items relating to the railway including one of its 2-6-4T locomotives. Perhaps in the future, the real Donegal Town station may see some of the activity and colour seen here on this layout.**

Opposite page, bottom: **Railcars Nos 12 and 14 and trailer No 3 are seen at Castlefinn station on another part of this layout.** Both, Andy Cundick

Photographs on this page:
Top left: **This 4mm scale model of a Clogher Valley Railway bogie Composite coach was built from a Branchlines etched brass kit.**

Top right: **This 4mm scale model of a CVR horse box was also made from a Branchlines etched brass kit.**

Above: **Here, examples of wagons from two different Irish 3ft gauge systems are seen together. On the left is a WCR open wagon and on the right an LLSR van. Both have bodies made from marine plywood. The van is on a modified Berlin-Bahnen wagon chassis. The running gear of the open wagon uses cast components made for 3mm scale modelling.**
All three photos, Alan O'Rourke

Below: **This model of a Tralee & Dingle Railway 2-6-0T in 4mm scale was built from a Branchlines kit. Several of these T&D 2-6-0Ts were transferred to the Cavan & Leitrim line after the final closure of the T&D in 1953, so this model could be used as well for a layout based on the C&L in its later years.** Alan O'Rourke

Above: **Working in the larger scales allows a high degree of realism. This model of a Castlederg & Victoria Bridge Tramway van is in 15mm scale and runs on 45mm gauge track. The model is made from strip wood, ply and some commercial components designed for 16mm scale modelling.** Neil Ramsay

Below: **This model of an LLSR three compartment bogie Brake third in 4mm scale was built using the cut down sides from an old Tri-ang OO Brake clerestory coach running on modified Berliner-Bahnen bogies. Although the latter LLSR carriage livery was drab grey, in the early days the company used an attractive two tone salmon and brown scheme, similar to that used on the English L&SWR, which this model displays.** Alan O'Rourke

CHAPTER 7

MODELLING IN FINESCALE

We have all heard the term 'finescale' used in relation to model railways. So what exactly is meant by this term and does it have any relevance to modelling Irish Railways? Basically, the term is applied to the relationship between the wheels and track of a model and it does have some importance for Irish modellers. For those who model in 4mm scale for instance, we have quite a choice of what standard we can use: OO, EM or P4. Most modellers are aware that these different standards come in different gauges, namely 16.5mm, 18.2mm and 18.83mm respectively. However, this is only part of the story. The gauge used and wheel and track standards are in fact two completely separate issues. These different standards relate to how accurately the wheel and track dimensions are reproduced in model form. The main measurements of concern are wheel tyre width, flange depth, back to back clearances (the distance between the backs of the wheels), gauge, check clearance and flange width. OO standards are the coarsest whilst P4 standards are the finest. Appendix 2 (see page 86) lists these measurements for the different standards in 4mm scale.

Many British and Irish modellers are quite happy to accept OO gauge standards using 16.5mm trackwork. There is nothing wrong with this and it is by far the easiest way of getting an Irish model up and running fairly quickly. However, the Irish broad gauge of 5ft 3in is quite wide and equates to a 4mm scale track gauge of 21mm. To some modellers, running Irish models on 16.5mm trackwork looks a bit odd, especially if there are adjacent 3ft gauge tracks. Consequently, they have tried to reproduce their trackwork to the correct gauge. This involves building all the trackwork and modifying the rolling stock to suit. Components for track building are readily available from specialist suppliers and societies and it is not as difficult as it may at first seem. The first thing to decide is what standard to use, as it is possible to build Irish broad gauge 21mm track using OO, EM or P4 standards. Most Irish modellers who have decided to use 21mm gauge track have opted to use P4 standards. The basis for this is that if you are going to build your own track, you might as well try and get it as near as possible. All the components for building the track are readily available and the job is made easier by the fact that a number of gauges are made to ease construction.

Left: **The difference in gauge between the 16.5mm (left) and 21mm gauges (right) can be seen in comparing these two wagons. MJT compensated wagon suspension has been used on the 21mm wagon.** Stephen Johnson

Another advantage of building one's own track is that it gives modellers the choice to tailor-make track formations to suit their particular requirements rather than try and make standard trackwork items fit the desired layout. However, the use of finer wheel standards creates another problem. It follows that if the flanges are not as deep as OO, then the track will have be built and laid to a higher standard to avoid any vertical variations that could cause derailments by the flanges riding up onto the surface of the rails. Fortunately, there is a way around this, achieved by using suspension.

Rolling stock

The use of a suspension system on rolling stock is strongly advised if using P4 standards, and desirable if using EM standards. The aim of suspension is simply to keep all the wheels of the vehicle in contact with the track at all times. This sounds obvious enough, but with a flange depth of less than 1mm in P4, it doesn't take too much to de-rail a vehicle that is not fitted with some sort of suspension. There are many ways to achieve this and numerous products are available commercially. In the case of carriages and wagons, most of these can be easily modified or can have some form of suspension included when they are being built. When it comes to locomotives, however, especially steam locomotives, this is more problematical and they often have to have a purpose built sprung chassis. So, in considering modelling in a more accurate standard, the modeller will have to accept that they will have to build all the trackwork and modify, or purpose build, the running units of the rolling stock. This can appear to be a daunting task, but it really isn't as difficult as it may sound and the results can be quite impressive.

Building the track

The first thing to consider is how one is going to build the track. The simplest method is to use PCB trackwork, where one solders lengths of rail onto pre-cut PCB strips. This is a very popular method

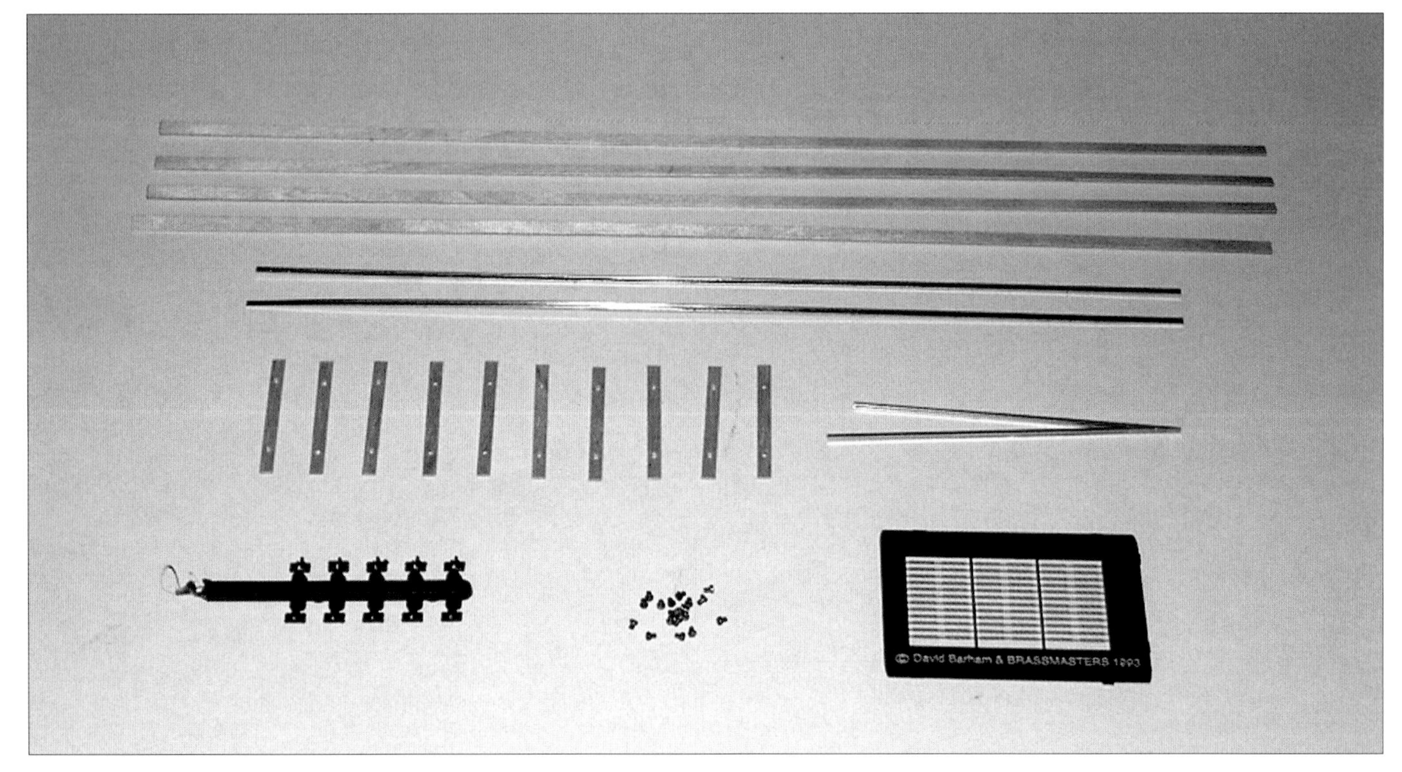

Above: **This view shows a selection of the parts used in track construction. Included are; point sleepering (top), machined point blades (middle), pre-punched ply sleepers (middle left), a pre-fabricated crossing 'V' (middle right), chairs (bottom left), rivets (bottom centre), and etched brass fishplates (bottom right).** Stephen Johnson

and is used extensively in EM or for the more adventurous OO modeller looking for that more unusual track formation. There are a number of suppliers who sell the components to make PCB trackwork. The most essential item one needs is a set of track gauges. These usually consist of a couple of tools for setting the overall gauge, one to set the running rail to check rail distance and another to set the flangeway width through a point or crossing. Templates for a variety of points and crossings are also available. However, these are usually for British standard gauge and the modeller will have to allow for the wider Irish gauge during construction. One of the more difficult parts of constructing trackwork revolves around the components used in a point or crossing. The crossing 'V' needs to be fabricated from two sections of rail carefully filed down to produce the correct angle and the blades, or switch rails, also need to be filed down precisely. After a bit of practice, one can usually build a straightforward point in a couple of hours. For those who are not confident, at least one supplier sells ready prepared crossing 'V's and switch rails.

However, this method does not include some of the obvious features found in trackwork, such as the chairs and fishplates. To include this sort of detail, different methods are employed. One longstanding and popular method is ply and rivet construction. With this method, strips of thin plywood are cut to the correct length for the sleepers and two holes are punched through them. A small brass rivet is inserted through each hole and the open end peened back. The rails are then carefully soldered to the surface of the rivets, with the use of gauges, to produce the basic track. In a straight or curved piece of trackwork, it is not necessary to solder the rails to all the sleepers, but rather every fourth or fifth will suffice. Commercially available moulded chairs can also be used in a cosmetic function to complete the effect. A variety of different chairs are available ranging from two bolt to four bolt

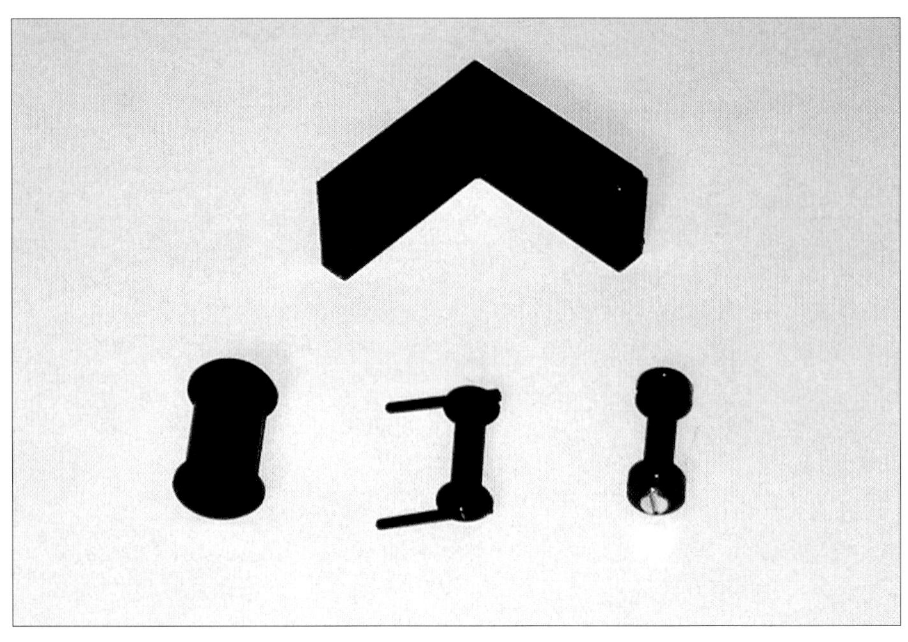

Left: **A selection of Brooke Smith gauges for 21mm P4 track construction. Included are; a back-to-back gauge (top), a rolling track gauge (left), checkrail (middle) and flangeway gauge (right).** Stephen Johnson

chairs. Track panels can be made up with etched brass or plastic cosmetic fishplates. The Scalefour Society produces ready-made plywood sleepers, a scale 8ft 6in in length, with the holes prepunched for Irish standard gauge. The same society also supplies the rivets, rails and a set of gauges.

Another system is produced by Exactoscale Ltd and uses a set of jigs and gauges to produce track formations in a slightly different way to the ply and rivet method. Ready machined crossing 'V's and switch rails are also available to aid construction from other suppliers such as C & L Finescale Ltd. Either method produces quite excellent-looking trackwork. Details on how to construct track using the ply and rivet method can be found in Iain Rice's excellent book, *An Approach to Building Finescale Trackwork in 4mm*, published by Wild Swan. Details on the Exactoscale Ltd system may be obtained directly from the supplier.

Wheels and axles

Suitable wheels for P4 and EM standards are now quite easy to obtain, either from the specialist societies or from commercial manufacturers such as Ultrascale, Alan Gibson, Sharman and Exactoscale to mention a few. Axles can be more difficult because of the wider gauge. Most of these suppliers manufacture items for British prototypes and consequently the axles tend to be too short. Pin point wagon and carriage axles are usually 26mm long, whereas the 21mm broad gauge modeller requires an axle 28mm long. Ultrascale will supply their wheels on the correct length axles and from time to time, smaller suppliers make and supply a batch. Alternatively, one can make one's own from 2mm diameter silver steel rod. Steam locomotive wheels tend to use ⅛in axles and again, those supplied in the pack will be too short. The solution is to make one's own from ⅛in silver steel rod cut to the correct length. Silver steel rod in various diameters is available from suppliers such as Eileen's Emporium. Diesel locomotives seem to use either 2mm axles or ⅛in axles depending on type and manufacturer. One essential tool required here is a back-to-back gauge, used to set the distance between the inside faces of the wheels. This is quite important and needs to be accurately set otherwise the wheels will either not sit on the track properly, if they are too wide, or will catch the checkrails on points and crossings, if too narrow. Checking these gauges is, however, not a difficult job.

Suspension

Suspension, or compensation as it is usually called, is an essential feature of P4 standards and to a lesser degree EM. The use of finer standard wheels with their smaller flange depth increases the possibility of a vehicle leaving the track over slight vertical imperfections. Over the years, a number of solutions to the problem have appeared. The simplest form used in wagon construction is the 'rocking W-iron' system. For a four-wheel wagon, one would keep one axle and wheelset fixed whilst allowing the other set to rock slightly. This is achieved by using a fold up brass etch with the W-irons represented at the ends. Brass wheel bearings are inserted in the holes in the W-iron and the complete wheelset runs in this frame. The frame is fixed to the wagon by means of a pivot which allows the assembly to rock up and down to compensate for variations in the track. The W-iron can then be fitted with cosmetic detail such as axle-boxes and springs. Studio Scale Models produce etches for rocking W-irons in 21mm gauge for outside pin points whereas MJT supply some internal bearing types that can be used for the wider gauge. One advantage with the inside bearing type is that little or no modification to the W-irons is needed, other than to make sure there is sufficient clearance. The disadvantage is the increased friction compared to pin points. Another method that has gained popularity in recent years is the fixed axleguard system. Here, the W-irons are fixed but the axles can slide up and down the hornguide, just like the real thing. The advantage here is that all the wheels are sprung and there is less clutter under the wagon. Such a system is offered by Exactoscale Ltd, who will supply suitable 28mm axles on request.

Carriages and other bogie vehicles use a different system. The simplest and easiest is a carriage compensation unit (CCU) as produced by MJT. In this system, a bogie is made up from two fold-up brass etches soldered together with a piece of brass wire. The brass wire acts like a torsion bar and allows the two halves to twist slightly. The bogies are fixed to the underside of the vehicles by means of press studs. One bogie is allowed to move freely in all directions whereas the other is limited laterally. The result is a three point suspension system. This works particularly well and the EM/P4 etches are easily modified for the Irish broad gauge by using a longer torsion bar. Dummy sideframes are fitted to the unit to complete the bogie. Another system is similar to the fixed axleguard wagon system, where a rigid frame is used and the axles move in the hornguides.

Right: **This view illustrates the difference between a Bachmann 16mm OO gauge wheelset (left) and an Ultrascale 21mm gauge P4 wheelset.**
Stephen Johnson

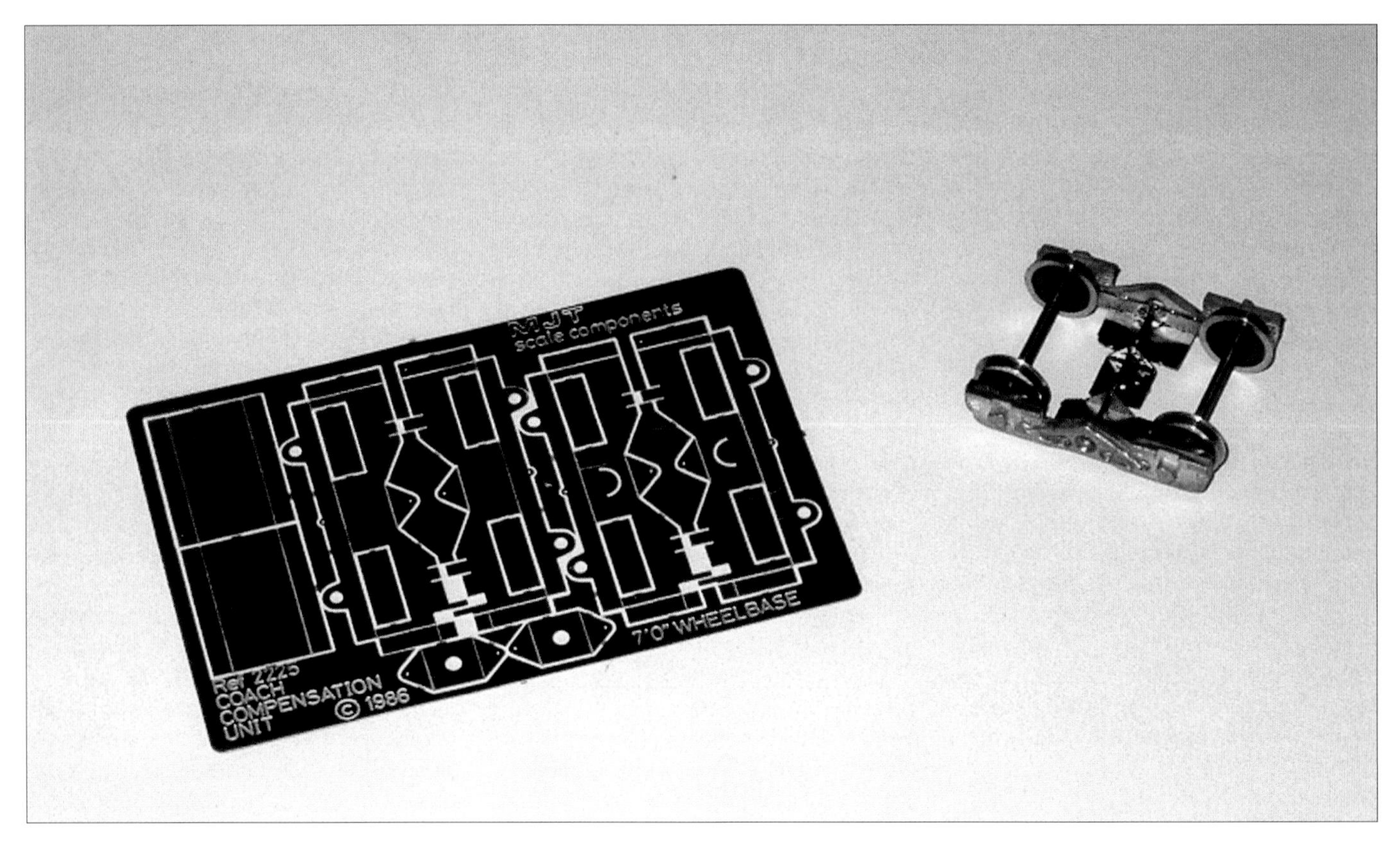

Above: **The MJT type carriage compensation unit is supplied on an etched brass fret (left) in various wheelbases. To the right is a 21mm gauge bogie for a CIÉ fertiliser wagon using the MJT CCU, although some of the etch had to be cut away to make it less visible behind the white metal sideframes.** Stephen Johnson

One advantage with some of the above systems is that the brake blocks can be fixed to the suspension unit with the block placed very close to, and in line with, the wheel tread without fear of touching. Such positioning of the brake shoes gives a more realistic appearance. For six-wheeled stock, Brassmasters make etches for compensating units which can be built to a variety of wheelbases.

Locomotives can be rather more complicated, depending on what is being built. In a basic four or six coupled steam locomotive, one axle, usually the driven one, is kept fixed whilst the others are allowed some vertical movement. One method is to use a beam pivoted between the moving axles and resting on the axles. Another method is to use sprung hornblocks. Obviously, with both these systems, the connecting rods cannot be one piece. Diesel locomotives can be easier. Many people use commercially available running units and some of these have an amount of vertical play anyway. One popular make of chassis is produced by the American company Athearn. These chassis can be easily re-gauged and the small amount of vertical play seems to be about enough. Converting OO gauge steam engines can result in a few more problems. Take the Bachmann Woolwich Mogul for instance. New, longer axles would be required in addition to a new set of wheels. The frames would have to be built up to fill the gap left by the broader gauge and cylinders moved out. You would be lucky to find a set of P4 standard wheels with the same throw on the crank and distance from the centre of the axle, which could result in building a new set of valve gear! However, most modellers prefer to build a model from one of the many kits now on the market, where the broader gauge and compensation can be built in from the start.

Other features

Many 'finescale' modellers use the opportunity to add more realistic detail to their models. One common feature is couplings. Many of us have started off with the familiar Hornby-type tension lock coupling. This is a reliable and robust design, but has a number of shortcomings. The first problem is its size. Although the tension lock has got smaller over the years, it is still rather on the large side. The other problem concerns uncoupling. A special uncoupling ramp tends to be used, usually made out of brown plastic, a little unsightly and hardly prototypical. Some modellers have tried to alleviate the problem by using a strip of clear acetate sheet. The most prototypical coupling one could use is a proper screw or three-link coupling. These are available from a number of suppliers, Exactoscale Ltd probably being the best, but are fiddly and require the 'Hand of God' reaching down with a hook to couple and uncouple stock. Various solutions have been proposed to overcome this problem over the years such as the Spratt & Winkle type, the Dingham, the DG and the Alex Jackson type. They all offer remote coupling and uncoupling, uncoupling achieved by a discreet under baseboard electro-magnet. One simply energises the electro-magnet, usually by a push button switch, as the stock to be uncoupled passes over it. The stock can then continue being pushed back to the required location. When the train moves forward again, it leaves the uncoupled stock in situ. The Spratt & Winkle type is quite popular but does require a largish hook and a piece of wire attached across the buffer heads, which somewhat defeats the object of producing realistic-looking stock. The Dingham and DG couplings work on a similar principle using a small loop and hook. They are more discreet than the Spratt & Winkle type but do limit the amount of buffer beam detail possible on a modern diesel locomotive. By far the best is the Alex Jackson or AJ type. This uses a fine spring steel wire, the end of which is bent to form a special hook. No 11 guitar wire (0.011in diameter or 32swg) is quite suitable material for this. The coupling is very discreet, almost invisible in some situations, allowing full buffer beam detail. Uncoupling is achieved by using a small iron or steel dropper, hidden behind a wheel, which is pulled downwards under the attraction of an electro-magnet. A special jig is available from Martins' Model Accessories or the EM Gauge Society to assist with making the coupling. There are a few minor disadvantages though. The stock cannot be easily coupled up on curves and the setting of the coupling can be fiddly, but the final look is well worth it. In some cases, modellers have fitted three-link or screw couplings to a rake of stock that would not normally be broken and used one of the specialist remote couplings at the end of the rake. For narrow gauge modellers, Branchlines produce a working Chopper Coupling.

Another feature 'finescale' modellers fit is working sprung buffers. A number of different patterns are offered by a few manufacturers, some of which are suitable for Irish modellers. They are fairly easy to fit and do look good as a locomotive backs up onto a train and compresses the buffers. There is a more practical aspect to sprung buffers when using the Alex Jackson coupling though. When pushing a train, the AJ coupling prototypically relies on the buffers making contact and transmitting the force, unlike the other types of coupling which transmit the force through the coupling. When stock is set back through a curve, one buffer will compress slightly and will help prevent binding and buffer lock. One important point about buffers on Irish prototypes is that they are set further apart than their British counterparts, at 6ft 3in centres.

Finescale or not

The building or conversion of stock to 'finescale' standards, whether OO, EM or P4 is not the easiest task in the world, but neither is it the most difficult. Some modellers will always prefer to get a model out of the box and run it on commercial track, which is absolutely fine. Others though, like to try and get things looking just that little bit better. We hope that these notes will have informed and interested you rather than put you off. After all, you only get out of a hobby what you put in. If you are interested in pursuing this aspect of model building, then membership of one of the specialist societies such as the EM Gauge Society (EMGS) or Scalefour Society is very useful. The *EMGS Manual* and *Scalefour Digest* are invaluable reference aids and provide a lot of useful information. They also supply some of the more specialised parts that your local model shop will probably not stock. It is well worth looking out for some EM or P4 layouts at model railway exhibitions. The techniques are all the same even if the gauge isn't and the exhibitors are usually very happy to answer any questions you may have. Ultimately it is up to the individual to decide what they would like to do and how far to go. As long as you are happy with what you are doing, then that's what counts!

Below: **This illustrates two of the couplings referred to in the text. The wagon on the left is fitted with a DG coupling whilst that on the right has an Alex Jackson type coupling.**
Stephen Johnson

CHAPTER 8

GALLERY

Above: **One of the joys of railway modelling is that each individual can set his own standards. Unless he chooses to display his models in public, the only criteria for success are that the building and running of the models give him pleasure. There are, however, some gifted and skilful individuals who practice modelling to very high standards. Even if we are not all able to emulate them, their work is a constant source of inspiration. In this section of the book, we provide a gallery of some of this work in our field which shows just what can be done. We start with this model of the GNR's only diesel locomotive. The Hobbytrain model of the Deutsche Bundesbahn V 65 is not dissimilar to the MAK eight-wheel diesel acquired by the GNR Board in 1954 and numbered 800. At the dissolution of the GNRB, this machine came to CIÉ who renumbered it K801. With a few minor modifications to the body and a repaint, a pleasing model may be made of this unique locomotive, although it should be remembered that it is 3.5mm; 1ft scale.** Stephen Johnson

Opposite page, bottom: **At one time, MTK produced a large range of kits of irish prototypes. One of these was a kit for a push-pull train based on the AEC/Park Royal railcars. This particular model has been modified to return the vehicle to its original powered railcar configuration.**

Right: **The railbus, that most Irish of vehicles, is most often associated with the GNR; however, this is a CIÉ example. No 2508 was converted from an AEC Regal road bus. The vehicle was normally used on the now-closed Thurles to Clonmel line. The model uses a Lledo die-cast bus body mounted on a Tenshodo motor bogie.** Both, Stephen Johnson

Below: **GNR T2 class 4-4-2T No 69 was built in 1983 to finescale by David Malone to run on 21mm gauge track, from a TMD kit. The model is finished in GNR black livery but is weathered to show how the livery would gradually discolour in service.** David Malone

CONNAUGHT
48
M. G. W. R.

C N R
C
16

379

Photos on the opposite page:

Top: **This model of a MGWR 'D' class 2-4-0 was scratch-built in brass by David Malone in 4mm scale, 21mm gauge. The locomotive is fitted with tender drive through a Studiolith (now known as Exactoscale) 2:1 gearbox via a wire shaft to a Studiolith worm gear on the rear axle of the engine.** David Malone

Middle: **GNR(I) 'SG2' class 0-6-0 No 16 is built in 4mm scale for 21mm gauge. This started life as an SSM kit but has a fully compensated scratch-built chassis, with the drive by a 54:1 gearbox and Mashima 1620 motor and flywheel. All the boiler fittings, except the dome, are turned brass replacements.** Harry Byrne

Bottom: **CIÉ 'K' class 2-6-0 No 379 is another 4mm scale/21mm gauge model, essentially scratch-built but incorporating boiler and cab side sheets from a Will cast kit for the SECR/SR version of these engines. The model retains the SECR style chimney. No 379 is thought to be the only one of the prototype engines with 5ft 6in driving wheels, which retained this feature.** Harry Byrne

Photos on this page:

Above: **This model of GNR 'SG3' class 0-6-0 No 47 in 4mm scale/21mm gauge, was scratch-built by Terry MacDermott, utilising the fully compensated chassis from the SSM 'SG2' class kit. Drive is to the rear axle by a SSM 50:1 gear mount from a Mashima 1620 motor.** Harry Byrne

Bottom: **The original CIÉ 'J30' class 0-6-0T No 90, is one of the all too few Irish broad gauge steam locomotives which have been preserved. This model of the locomotive in 4mm scale/21mm gauge, was originally built by Tim Cramer and subsequently came into the possession of Harry Byrne. Recently, it has had an extensive rebuild with a new compensated chassis including an 80:1 gearbox and a Mashima 1220 motor and flywheel. An interesting feature of the rebuild is the fitting of correctly shaped sprung buffers which because of the lack of space behind the buffer beams have internal springs, completely housed within the barrel of the buffer beam.** Harry Byrne

Left: **Large scale garden lines can be incredibly atmospheric as the two views on this page, of 15mm scale 45mm gauge models, demonstrate. This model of an ex-Ballymena & Larne Railway 2-4-0T, in LMS/NCC livery made by David Bailey of DJB Engineering, is based on his models of the similar engines built by Beyer, Peacock, which ran on the Isle of Man. The model runs on methylated spirits.**

Below: **Cavan & Leitrim 4-4-0T No 8 was built by Stuart Brown of Archangel with detailing and weathering by Neil Ramsay. The locomotive is fired by butane gas and has slip eccentric reversing gear.** Both, Neil Ramsay

Right: **A close up look at the business end of a representative of the last new class of 5ft 3in gauge locomotives to be delivered to the Irish railways. Whereas the bulk of the General Motors built '201' class went to CIÉ/IR, two were supplied to NIR to work the Dublin to Belfast 'Enterprise Express' services. This 4mm version of No 210 was built by Stephen Johnson for his Dunmore & Fidlin layout.** Stephen Johnson

Below: **GNR S class 4-4-0 No 171 *Slieve Gullion* is another of the few Irish 5ft 3in gauge steam locomotives to have been preserved. The model, built by Harry Byrne and finished in the Great Northern's glorious lined blue livery by Brian Badger, is essentially an SSM kit with a compensated scratch-built chassis.** Harry Byrne

Right: **Tralee & Dingle Hunslet built 2-6-2T No 5 is a live steam model by Archangel in 16mm scale, though running on the technically too narrow O gauge track. The model was also produced in a version to run on 45mm track. It has steel frames, the pony truck wheels are sprung with piano wire and the leading and trailing coupled wheels have coil springs. The working Walschaerts valve gear drives a rigid centre axle.The engine has a pot boiler, externally fired with methylated spirits. The dome, which conceals the boiler filler cap, and the chimney are made from brass. The engine works at a boiler pressure of about 60lbs per square inch. One boiler fill will allow for a 30 to 60 minute running session, depending on the weather, although the meths burner needs more frequent replenishment.** Ian Lawrence

Above: **GSR No 800 *Maedb* was built by George Hanan in 7mm scale in the early 1970s using drawings made by Cyril Fry. The livery of this particular model is genuine GSR green. The paint used to finish the model was part of a small supply obtained by Fry from Inchicore in 1939.** John Brennan

Left: **Virtually all the locomotives at work in Ireland today are the products of the American General Motors Company. The first General Motors class to be introduced consisted of the 15 single cab 950hp machines delivered in 1961. As new they were turned out in an attractive grey and yellow livery but they were soon repainted in the then new CIÉ black and tan colours. This is the livery carried by B127, made from a MIR kit, seen here on duty at Dunmore & Fidlin station.** Stephen Johnson

Below left: **In the 1970s Harry Connaughton made this model of Great Northern 'JT' class 2-4-2T No 95 in 4mm scale, to run on 21mm gauge track. It now runs on an EM mechanism supplied by Eric Robinson.** Alan O'Rourke

Opposite page, centre: **This model of CIÉ 'J15' class 0-6-0 No 184, another locomotive which has been preserved, is in 4mm scale to run on 21mm gauge track. It was built by Harry Byrne using a much modified SSM kit with a scratch-built chassis. In order to keep the cab clear for backhead details and to have daylight under the boiler, drive is onto the leading axle by a modified Exactoscale 38:1 gearbox using a flexible coupling to a 1224 Mashima motor fitted with a flywheel.** Harry Byrne

Opposite page, bottom: **GNR 'P' class 4-4-0 No 73 *Primrose* was built by Philip Preston in 7mm scale. The model, which even has working inside valve gear, shows the locomotive in the lined green livery it carried before the Great War.** John Brennan

Right: **GSWR 2-4-0 N0 273, acquired by that company with its takeover of the Waterford, Limerick & Western who had named the locomotive *Galtee More*, has been turned out in the olive green livery used by the GSWR before World War 1. The painting and lining on the model is the handiwork of Ian Rathbone.** John Brennan

001
001
001

Opposite page, top: **The CIÉ Metropolitan-Vickers 'A' class locomotives are one of the most popular diesels to have run on irish railways. This is a 4mm, 21mm gauge, P4 model, made from the Q Kits white metal kit, running on a re-gauged Airfix Class 31 chassis. The model is finished in the 1980s variation of the CIÉ black and tan livery. By this time the prototypes had lost their original and rather unreliable power units and had been re-engined with General Motors diesel engines.** Stephen Johnson

Opposite page, bottom: **The realism that can be obtained with large scales and live steam is well illustrated in this view of the ex-Ballymena & Larne 2-4-0T, modelled in its later LMS/NCC livery, in action.** Neil Ramsay

This page, above: **A former Cork, Blackrock & Passage 2-4-2T, in its later guise as Cavan & Leitrim section No 10L passes over the river bridge next to the church on Charles Insley's Cahir Patrick layout. The chassis is based on that from a Grafar LMS compound.**

This page, right: **A view of the main street in Cahir Patrick. The model maker has taken great pains to put so much interesting detail into this street scene. Sometimes modellers focus so much on the locomotives and the rolling stock that other aspects of the layout tend to suffer. This is certainly not the case in this instance as witnessed by this delightful street scene.** Both Tony Wright, courtesy British Railway Modelling

FINE
GUINNES
IS GOOD
FOR YOU

Opposite page:

Top: **Some more views of that splendid recreation of the irish 3ft gauge, the Cahir Patrick layout, grace these pages. CDR railcar No 8 rests in the engine shed at Cahir Patrick. The model is scratch-built from Plasticard and runs on a Grafar DMU motor bogie.**

Below: **Cavan & Leitrim No 4L rounds the curve on the approach to Cahir Patrick with a C&L clerestory coach and some goods wagons in tow.**

This page:

Above: **A close up view of Cahir Patrick station.**

Right: **Ireland offers many unusual prototypes that can be modelled. None more so than the last steam locomotive built for the Irish broad gauge, Oliver Bulleid's CC1, more commonly referred to as the 'Turf Burner', an attempt to find a way to use Ireland's only indigenous fuel, turf or peat, for rail traction. This fine model of the locomotive, made to P4 standards by Dennis Bates, performs a good deal better than the prototype. The locomotive is seen at work on Tony Miles' Adavoyle Junction layout.** All photographs on pages 78 and 79, Tony Wright, courtesy British Railway Modelling

Above: **We offer two views of Harry Mulholland's excellent 7mm scale Great Northern layout, Knockmore Junction, on this page. The GNR weedkiller train comes off the Antrim branch and trundles along the main line in the direction of Belfast, past Knockmore Junction signal cabin.**

Right: **Work on the permanent way at Knockmore Junction is halted to allow GNR SG2 class 0-6-0 No 16 and its train of new cars to pass along the main line towards Belfast. The line to the left led on the prototype to Banbridge and ultimately to Newcastle, with GNR trains exercising running powers over part of the BCDR system to reach that destination.** Both, Tony Wright, courtesy of British Railway Modelling

Above: **The Great Northern in all its glory in 4mm scale on the Adavoyle Junction layout. GNR 'V' class compound 4-4-0 No 86 *Peregrine* arrives at Adavoyle Junction station resplendent in its GNR sky blue livery, hauling a set of teak liveried coaches.** Tony Wright, courtesy British Railway Modelling

Below: **Whereas there is still definitely a predominant preference for steam era rather than modern traction layouts in Britain, perhaps because dieselisation came so early on the CIÉ system, many more modellers of the Irish scene look to the post steam era for their inspiration. Some of the early CIÉ diesel classes have also had a very long innings which means that the same locomotive can appear in layouts covering a period from the 1960s through to the new century, with perhaps just a change of livery. One such class is the General Motors '141' class Bo-Bo diesels which were ordered in 1962. These were mechanically similar to the earlier '121' class but had a cab at both ends. One of the first batch, No 150, is seen at Dunmore & Fidlin station in the 1990s IR livery.** Stephen Johnson

BALLYCLARE

Opposite page:

Top: **The influence of the LMS can readily be seen as a NCC 'W' class Mogul arrives at Ballyclare with a passenger train. To the left is one of the two NCC 'Y' class 0-6-0Ts. These engines began their working lives across the Irish Sea on the 4ft 8½in gauge. The two LMS '3Fs', commonly known as 'Jinties' were re-gauged and sent over to Northern Ireland in 1944 to help with the huge volume of additional traffic which World War 2 had brought to the NCC system.**

Below: **Diesel traction came early in Northern Ireland and well as to the south. The UTA led the way in early DMU development and many of its ideas were incorporated into early British Railways designs. Two of the UTA's Multi-Purpose-Diesels (MPDs), on the right No 32 and on the left No 64, stand at Newcastle station. As well as working passenger trains, the MPDs were used to haul goods trains.** Both, Tony Wright, courtesy British Railway Modelling

This page:

Above: **Noel Dodd's modern image layout is centred on Greystones station. A '141' class No 177 and a re-engined Metrovick locomotive are on permanent way trains at Greystones.** Tony Wright, courtesy British Railway Modelling

Right: **We began this book with references to the pioneering work of Cyril Fry whose models are now housed at Malahide Castle in a permanent exhibition. This part of the layout is a model of the former GSWR Glanmire Road station in Cork,.** Courtesy Dublin Tourism

Left: **Inspired by the work of Cyril Fry, the vast layout at Malahide Castle is a 'must see' attraction for all of those interested in railway modelling. The visitor is led around the exhibition by a commentary with various parts of the layout being illuminated as one progresses. It covers virtually the whole history of Ireland's railways on both the country's two main gauges. Dublin's first generation tramways and even a cross channel ferry also get a look in. The main stations in Dublin, Belfast and Cork are modelled as are many of the most famous features of the Irish network such as the Boyne viaduct at Drogheda and, in this view, the loop line bridge over the Liffey linking Connolly and Tara Street stations in the centre of Dublin city. This corner of the layout features also Dublin's Heuston station, barges on the River Liffey, the electrified DART network and a variety of buses and trams. Trains in different liveries, hauled by appropriate model motive power, ranging from the age of steam to the present day scene, move round the tracks in an ever-changing procession.**

Below: **Trains on both the 5ft 3in and 3ft gauges are seen on another part of the Fry Model Railway. The distinctive red livery of the CDR predominates in the foreground with both railcars and steam locomotives in view, whilst on the overhead lines behind, steam and diesel era goods trains pass by. The layout at Malahide is under continuous development. New rolling stock is added on a regular basis and scenic and operational features are also constantly being improved.** Both photographs, courtesy Dublin Tourism

APPENDIX ONE

IRISH MODEL MANUFACTURERS

Alphagraphix
23 Darris Road, Selly Park, Birmingham B29 7YQ.
E-mail: rogeralphagrafix@tiscali.co.uk
Card and resin kits for buildings and rolling stock in 4mm and 7mm scales, including the Tyrconnel range.

Backwoods Miniatures
11 Netherton Southside, Netherton Morpeth, Northumberland NE65 7EZ.
E-mail: sales@backwoods.dabsol.co.uk
Web site: http://www.backwoods.dabsol.co.uk
Kits for 4mm narrow gauge locomotives, railcars, coaches and wagons.

Brassmasters
PO Box 1137, Sutton Coldfield, West Midlands B76 1FU.
Etched brass kits and components including compensated six-wheel coach chassis.

Chivers Finelines
49 St Christine's Avenue, Leyland Preston, Lancs PR5 2YS
3.5m and 7mm kits for Tralee & Dingle 2-6-0T.

Exactoscale Ltd
29 Crouchmore Avenue, Esher, Surrey KT10 9AS. Tel: 0208 398 5818.
Web site: www.exactoscale.co.uk
Track, wheels, motors and other components.

EM Gauge Society
Mike Bell, 200A Prospect Road, Woodford Green, Essex IG8 7NG.
Web site: http://www/emgs.org

Frizinghall Model Railways
Model Railshop Dept, Frizinghall Models & Railways, 202 Keighley Road, Frizinghall, Bradford, West Yorkshire BD9 4JZ.
E-mail: modelrailshop@aol.com
Web site: http://secure.modelrailshop.co.uk/Irish_railways.html
Stockists of current ready-to-run commercial Irish models.

Alan Gibson
The Bungalow, Church Road, Lingwood, Norwich, Norfolk NR13 4TR.
Tel/fax: 01603 715862
Wheels, axles etc.

MJT (Mike Trice)
41 Oak Avenue, Shirley, Croydon CR0 8EP.
E-mail: modelrailshop@aol.com
Coach kits, bogies etc.

Model Irish Railways
12 Lyndale Grange, Kerman Road, Portadown, Co Armagh BT63 5XB.
Current IÉ and NIR locomotives, wagons, paints and transfers.

Model Signal Engineering
PO Box 70, Barton upon Humber DN18 5XY.
E-mail: andrew@modelsignals.com
Web site: http://www.modelsignals.com
Castings, etchings for building signals, wires lever frames etc for signal operation.

Murphy Models
Padraig Murphy, 2-4 Wexford Street, Dublin.
E-mail: murphymodels@eircom.net
Customised OO models.

Nonneminstre Models
42 Hide Gardens, Rustington, West Sussex BN16 3NP

No-nonsense Models
PO Box 1009, Cardiff CF23 7YB
Markets the MTK range, including modern image IÉ and NIR kits.

Northstar
Northstar Design, Llety Adar, Llanelian, Colwyn Bay LL29 6AT.
E-mail: adrianrowlandinwales@hotmail.com
10mm narrow gauge and 7mm broad gauge etched kits.

Parkside Dundas
Millie Street, Kirkcaldy, Fife KY1 2NL. Tel: 01592 640896.
4mm plastic kits for narrow gauge wagons (also market Ninelines kits).

Peco
Beer, Seaton, Devon EX12 3NA.
Web site: peco-uk.com
12mm gauge track for 3ft and metre gauge models in 3.5/4mm scale. Also supply Parkside Dundas and Ninelines kits.

Q Kits
43 St Mary's Avenue, Hemingbrough, Selby YO8 6YZ. Tel: 01757 630647.
CIE and NIR diesel models.

The Scalefour Society
Membership Secretary, Mr Brian Pearce, 5 Cedar Close, Teignmouth, Devon TQ14 8UZ
Web site: http://www.scalefour.org
Components for making 21mm gauge track

Sharman Wheels
13 Orwell Court, Wickford Business Park, Wickford, Essex.
Tel: 01268 764985. Fax: 011268 764985
E-mail: sales@sharmanwheels.co.uk
Web site: http://www.sharmanwheels.com
Wheels, gears, gearboxes

Studio Scale Models (has traded as TMD Models)
127 Otley Old Road, Lawnswood, Leeds LS16 6HH.
E-mail: paul.greene1@ntlworld.com
Cast and etched kits in 7mm, 4mm and S-scales.

Jeremy Suter
120 Hayurst Avenue, Middlewich, Cheshire CW10 0BD
4mm cast rolling stock kits.

Three MM Scale Model Railways
23 Gilbert Scott Road, Buckingham, Buckinghamshire MK18 1PS.
Tel: 01280 813860
Some components can be used for 12mm narrow gauge modelling in 4mm scale.

Ultrascale
Gear Services Letchworth, The Wynd East, Letchworth, Herts SG6 3EL
E-mail: gsl@ultrascale.co.uk
Web site: http://www.ultrascale.co.uk
Wagon and coach wheels on 28mm pin point axles for 21mm gauge.

Worsley Works
19 Douglas Road, Worsley M28 2SR
Web site: http://www.worsleyworks.freeserve.co.uk
Extensive range of 3ft kits in 3, 4, 5.5 and 7mm scale.

Alistair Wright (5522 Finescale Models)
The Coach House, The Hawthorns, Galashiels TD1 3NS. Tel: 01896 755509
E-mail: lms5522@netcomuk.co.uk
Coach kits and other components.

For those interested in live steam and the larger scales, there are other specialist suppliers such as Brandbright, Archangel and DJB Engineering, who advertise in magazines like *GardenRail*. Some of these companies make models suitable for Irish layouts.

APPENDIX TWO

WHEEL AND TRACK STANDARDS

Wheel and Track Standards for 4mm Scale 21mm Irish Broad Gauge

		OO Standards*	EM Standards†	P4 Standards‡
Flange Thickness	(FT)	0.65mm	0.65mm	0.35-0.4mm
Total Wheel Width	(TW)	2.28-2.5mm	2.28mm	2.28-2.5mm
Root Radius	(RR)	0.15mm	0.15mm	0.15mm
Coning Angle	(CA)	2°	2°	1 in 20
Back to Back	(BB)	19.2mm	19.3mm	19.84-19.92mm
Wheel Check Gauge	(WCG)	19.85-19.95mm	20.05mm	20.19-20.32mm
Track Gauge	(TG)	21-21.3mm	21mm	21mm
Permitted Gauge Widening	(PGW)	0.3mm @ 18in rad	0.2mm @ rad	0.22mm
Check Gauge	(CG)	20.1-20.2mm	20.05mm	20.32-20.37mm
Flangeway Width	(FW)	1.0mm	1.0mm	0.65-0.68mm
Check Clearance	(CC)	0.25mm	0.1mm	0.13-0.05mm
Running Clearance	(RC)	0.5mm	0.4mm	0.48-0.33mm

* Source, Iain Rice's suggested OO Finescale adjusted for 21mm gauge
† Source, EMGS Manual, adjusted for 21mm gauge
‡ Source, S4 Digest, adjusted for 21mm gauge

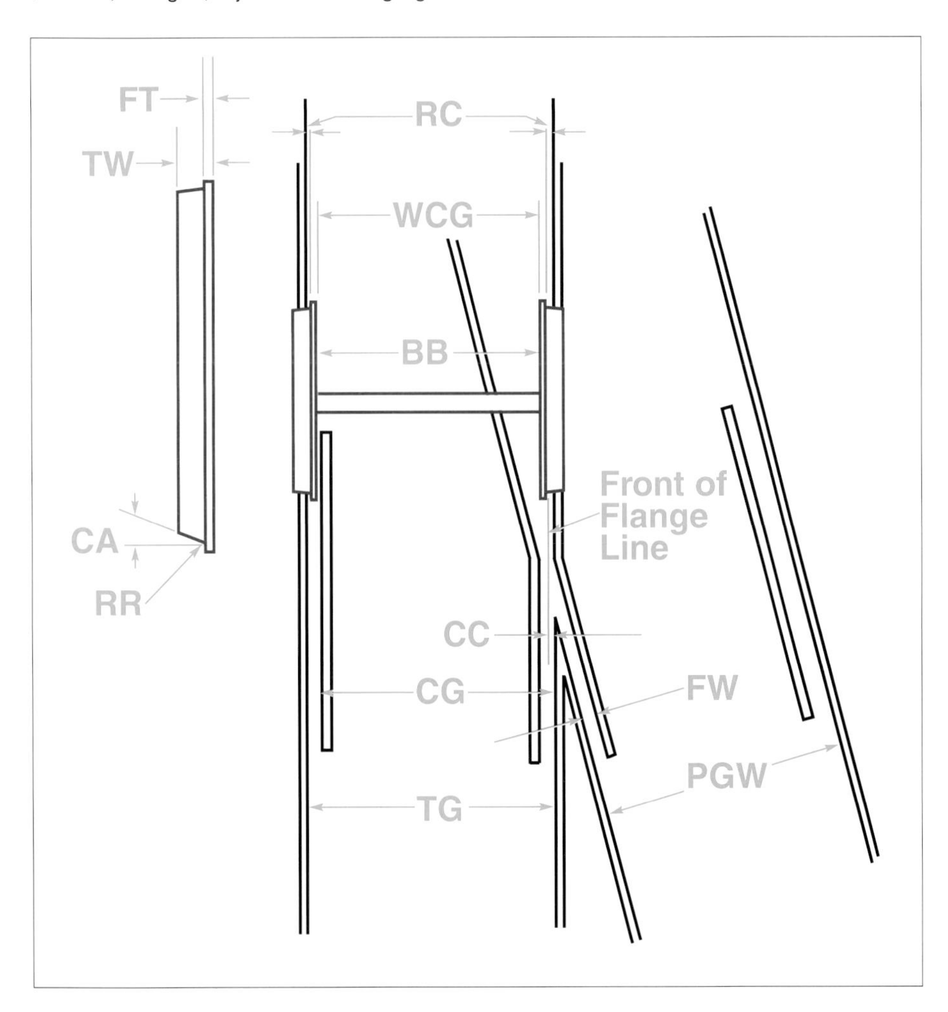

APPENDIX THREE

SOURCES OF INFORMATION

Societies and websites

The ***Irish Railway Record Society*** maintains an extensive library and archive in Dublin where there is a programme of meetings and library nights. There is also an active London area group which holds regular meetings. The IRRS publishes a journal three times annually and other occasional publications. Contact the society at, IRRS, Heuston Station, Dublin 8, Ireland. Website: http://www.irrs.ie/

The ***Railway Preservation Society of Ireland***, with bases at Whitehead and Mullingar, preserves and restores broad gauge locomotives and coaches for its rail tour programme. There is an annual journal and more frequent newsletters and e-newsletters to members and a programme of Winter meetings in Belfast. RPSI, PO Box 171, Larne, Co, Antrim Northern Ireland BT40 1UU. Website: http://www.rpsi-online.org/

The ***County Donegal Railway Restoration Limited***. The CDRRS website has extensive collections of archival material, especially on the CDR, LLSR and LBER systems. Website: http://www.county-donegalrailway.com

New Irish Lines is a newsletter published twice a year for Irish modellers, which is edited by this book's co-author Alan O'Rourke. It contains articles on prototypes and model construction, book and product reviews and information on drawing and photograph sources. The (2004) subscriptions is £5.00 per annum in Europe, £7.00 outside Europe. Contact, New Irish Lines, 72 Sandford Grove Road, Nether Edge Sheffield, England S7 1RR. E-mail: a.j.orourke@sheffield.ac.uk.

Irish Railway Modelling is an on-line discussion group hosted by Yahoo. http://groups.yahoo.com/group/Irishrailmodellers/

This book's co-author, Stephen Johnson has a website which includes an extensive Irish section, with resources and illustrated descriptions of models of many Irish engines, railcars, coaches and wagons. http://website.lineone.net/~sjohnson40/Irish%20lines.html

Sources for drawings

The first step in building an accurate model is tracking down good quality drawings. In addition to those which have been published in various books and magazine articles over the years, modellers may find the following archival collections useful. Please note that in many case these are original general arrangement engineering drawings, on large scales like 1in:1ft and very detailed, but for those with access to modern computer drawing packages, it should be possible to produce drawings for model making from such originals:

Metropolitan-Cammell: many Irish railway operators bought rolling stock from this company, or its constituents, in Birmingham. The archives include both large scale engineering drawings and makers' official photographs. Irish companies represented include the GSWR, MGWR, DWWR, WTR, WCIR, Dublin & Meath, GNR(I) and some narrow gauge lines. The collection is now in the care of the Historical Model Railway Society who are engaged in the process of cataloguing it For updates on the project see, http://www.hmrs.org.uk/news/03120101.shtml or contact, HMRS Drawings, Walden Villa, Pool Hill, Newent, Gloucestershire GL18 1LL.

The ***Public Records Office,*** Ruskin Avenue, Kew, Richmond. Tel: 081 876 3444. The main source of information is the Board of Trade files (MT6) which contain reports relating to the inspection of new lines. These contain detailed engineering reports, and in some cases there may be track or signalling diagrams, typically on a scale of 50ft:1in. Some files may include scale drawings of buildings, bridges and other features though finding these is rather pot luck. The PRO website is: http://www.pro.gov.uk/

Ulster Folk & Transport Museum, 153 Bangor Road, Cultra Holywood, Co Down, Northern Ireland BT18 0EU, website: http://www.uftm.org.uk

Many Irish companies acquired engines from British locomotive building firms. Beyer Peacock was the most prolific, of these building over 300 engines for service in Ireland. Many other suppliers were also active in building for the Irish companies. With the closure of these firms their drawings and in some cases the official works photographs have passed to museum collections. The following summarises the current location of these archives, though it should be noted that access may be limited by the needs of curatorial and conservation work. A good rule is to approach the relevant archivist for details of the current status of each collection.

Glasgow University Business Archives, Archives & Business Records Centre, University of Glasgow, 13 Thurso Street, Glasgow G12 8QQ. Tel: 041 339 8855 Ext. 6079. This is the repository for the records of the North British Locomotive Company (including some records from constituents like Dübs, Barclay and Neilson). It also has bound volumes of *The Engineer* and *Engineering*. There appear to be early Belfast & Ballymena, CBPR, Dublin & Belfast Junction, Dublin & Drogheda, Ulster and GSWR locomotive drawings here as well, but as with many archival collections, the indexing and cataloguing is still in progress. Drawings of a small number of GNR(I), MGWR, NCC, and GSWR can be inspected, and copies obtained.

Leeds Industrial Museum, Canal Road, Leeds LS12 2QF: general arrangement and detail drawings, registers and order books for the Avonside Engine Company (the National Railway Musuem at York also has copies of the order books) and drawings and records from Hudswell, Clarke & Co, the Hunslet Engine Company and Kerr, Stuart & Co.

Merseyside Maritime Museum, Department of Archives, Albert Dock, Liverpool L3 4AQ holds collections from the Vulcan Foundry, Newton-le-Willows, 1833-1904

(including works photographs) which lists early engines from the Cork & Bandon, Dublin & Wicklow, BCDR, WL&W and the Waterford & Central Ireland. Also found here are Robert Stephenson & Co and Robert Stephenson & Hawthorns Ltd photographs and general arrangement drawings. Enquiries should be directed to the Curator of Business Archives.

The Mitchell Library, North Street, Glasgow G3 7DN holds Dübs photographs and registers, Barclay photographs and Neilson photographs and registers.

Museum of Science & Industry in Manchester, Liverpool Road, Manchester M3 4FB is the custodian of the Beyer, Peacock archives, general arrangement and detail drawings, photographs, registers and order books. (The NRM at York also has copies of the order books.)

National Railway Museum, Library & Archive, Leeman Road, York YO26 4XJ holds the Dübs order books and general arrangement drawings, Hawthorne Leslie drawings and photographs, Naysmyth, Wilson & Co drawings and order books, Neilson drawings and order books and Peckett & Co drawings, photographs and registers.

Photographic collections

Just as important for accurate models as drawings is access to photographs, particularly when many Irish engines and much of the rolling stock underwent various modifications during their long lives.

Colour-Rail: 5 Treacher's Close, Chesham, Buckinghamshire, HP5 2HD offers a large collection of colour transparencies featuring Irish railways and tramways.

R S Carpenter: 407 Highter's Heath Lane, Hollywood, Birmingham B14 4TR issues lists and sells prints from the T R Perkins and Eddington collections and also can supply prints from the Lens of Sutton collection (see below).

The ***Historical Model Railway Society***: has a large collection, with a limited Irish content. Contact the HMRS's Photograph Sales Manager, 2 Poet's Corner, Westfield, Radstock, Bath BA23 2XZ.

The ***Kelland Photographic Collection*** is in the care of the Bournemouth Railway Society. List D covers the Irish lines and traction engines. Subjects covered include the BCDR, GSR, GNR(I), LLSR, NCC and SLNCR. The photographs are concentrated in the period 1928-1960, with the emphasis on locomotive portraits and action shots. Mr Mike Smith, Conishead, 5 Wren Crescent, Coy Pond, Branksome, Poole, Dorset BH12 1LB Tel: 01202 765545.

Lens of Sutton Collection: following the death of John L Smith (of Lens of Sutton fame) a voluntary group acquired his collection of some 75,000 negatives. So far, they have issued one Irish list (No 5), which has about 240 photographs of the BCDR, CMLR, CVBT, CBPR, CDR, DSER, DNGR, the West Cork lines, GSR, LLSR, NCC, MGWR, SSR, SLNC, TDR, WTR and WCR. Contact the Lens of Sutton Association, 8 Smiths Farm Lane, Didcot, Oxfordshire OX11 7DL.

The ***National Photographic Archive of Ireland*** includes the Lawrence, Valentine and Eason postcard collections from the late nineteenth/early twentieth centuries which include some railway scenes. The J P O'Dea Collection has a large railway content from 1938-77 period. The Morgan Collection offers aerial photographs from the mid-20th century, some of which show railway locations.

National Photographic Archive, Meeting House Square, Temple Bar, Dublin 2 Tel: (00 353) 01 6030 200, website: http://www.nli.ie/new_archive.htm. This now includes an on-line catalogue of the O'Dea Collection. The e-mail address is: photoarchive@nli.ie

The ***J F O'Neill Photographic Collection*** (Stephenson Locomotive Society, photographic list No 31) consists of a small, but interesting collection of 47 views taken on a trip to Ireland in July 1939. However, for a real treat, we will have to wait for the SLS to issue the catalogue for C G Camwell's work.

The ***Stephenson Photographic Collection***, contact K Greenwood, Bradstones, Charlton Road, Holcombe, Bath, Somerset BA3 5ER. Website: www.stephenson-loco.fsbusiness.co.uk/

The ***Ken Nunn Collection*** totals about 12,000 negatives, now in the care of the Locomotive Club of Great Britain. The Irish list covers about 450 shots, mostly from the 1914-1924 period, with a few going back to 1898. These are predominantly locomotive and train shots. Often, there are several similar shots taken close together, and helpfully the catalogue grades these from (a) (which are usually excellent) to (d) (which can be rather soft and streaked).

Contact the Locomotive Club of Great Britain through Graham Stacey, 11 Braywood Avenue, Egham, Surrey TW20 9LY.

Photos from the Fifties is an enormous and steadily expanding collection, with about 700 Irish shots mostly from the 1957-63 period, chiefly locomotive and train shots, but with a good selection of rolling stock and station views, including several narrow gauge and industrial systems. The proprietor runs a system where subscribers are sent regular update catalogues listing new and corrected entries. Contact, Hugh Davies, 32 Charterhouse Road, Godalming, Surrey GU7 2AQ Tel / fax: 01483 416357.

Stations UK specialises in location shots, showing station buildings and scenes, rather than the more usual locomotive and train views. For Ireland there is a single list, No 35, with about 1,400 entries from the period 1910-1975, although the majority are from the 1950-1965 period. About 150 of the pictures were taken in the 1930s. You do need to check what you are ordering as a number of the later pictures are taken after closure and thus may show the subjects in a derelict condition. Contact, Stations UK, 32 Birchdale Road, Waterloo, Merseyside, L22 9QX.

The well known railway writer ***Adrian Vaughan*** has a collection of locomotive and station views from the CIÉ period, including very good coverage of signalling equipment. He can be contacted at 13 The Street, Barney, Fakenham, Norfolk NR21 ONB

Finally, the ***Wycherley Photographic Collection*** has about 340 Irish pictures, mostly locomotive and shed scenes from the 1948-55 period. Contact R Baker, Photographic Archivist, Kidderminster Railway Museum, Station Approach, Comberton Hill, Kidderminster, Worcestershire DY10 1QX.